14: PERSPECTIVES IN CRITICISM

PERSPECTIVES IN CRITICISM

14:

Hilton Landry

Interpretations in Shakespeare's Sonnets

GREENWOOD PRESS, PUBLISHERS
WESTPORT, CONNECTICUT

Library of Congress Cataloging in Publication Data

Landry, Hilton.
   Interpretations in Shakespeare's sonnets.

   Reprint of the ed. published by the University of
California Press, Berkeley which was issued as no. 14
of Perspectives in criticism.
   Bibliography: p.
   Includes index.
   1. Shakespeare, William, 1564-1616. Sonnets.
I. Title. II. Series: Perspectives in criticism ; 14.
PR2848.L3 1976   822.3'3   76-1901
ISBN 0-8371-8749-4

Originally published in 1964 by University of California Press,
Berkeley

Reprinted with the permission of University of California
Press

Reprinted in 1976 by Greenwood Press,
a division of Congressional Information Service, Inc.
88 Post Road West, Westport, Connecticut 06881

Library of Congress catalog c___ _____ 76-1901
ISBN 0-8371-8749-4

Printed in the United States of America

10 9 8 7 6 5 4 3 2

To the memory of RHL

Preface

THERE IS no more unity in this work than in the Sonnets themselves; that is, there are recurrent principles and interests, but each chapter, as an attempt to interpret certain related poems, is comparatively independent. However, all the Sonnets I have chosen to discuss do contain difficulties or problems—even though they may only have been imported by commentators—which may be resolved by careful examination of the poems in the light of the proper contexts. In all but a few cases these contexts are provided by other Sonnets, usually adjacent ones. The opening chapter presents something of an archetypal example, and it is the conceptual matrix from which the succeeding chapters issue.

I have not said everything I could about any of the Sonnets: for the sake of clarity and economy I have merely sketched what seems to me to be the most probable interpretation and have often given short definitions of words and phrases. This has resulted in a flattening of meaning which may be inevitable in any attempt to discuss more than a few poems. My views on the Sonnets have been formed independently, but in a field to which so much time and talent has been dedicated, it is impossible to avoid the use of traditional wisdom. I have tried to acknowledge all the anticipations, parallels, and borrowings that I was aware of, and many of the notes constitute my tribute to those older editors like Tucker, Pooler, Wyndham, Dowden, and Beeching who provide many useful glosses on details. From the lectures and writings of I. A. Richards and Hyder Rollins I have learned more than mere words can convey.

I am indebted to the research committee of the University of California, Davis, for providing funds for the typing of the manuscript, and to the university administration for a faculty summer fellowship which enabled me to complete the final version. I am grateful to Harry Levin for valuable suggestions made at an early stage of the work, and to my good friend H. K. Gregory for his acute criticism of a number of my interpretations. My thanks are also due to my colleagues Everett Carter and Thomas Hanzo, who read and commented on the manuscript, and above all to my wife Elaine, who rendered invaluable assistance in many ways.

H. L.

Contents

'Twere well therefore if a careful and critical reader would first form to himself some plan, when he enters upon an author deserving a stricter inquiry: if he would consider that originals have a manner allways peculiar to themselves; and not only a manner, but a language: if he would compare one passage with another; for such authors are the best interpreters of their own meaning: and would reflect, not only what allowances may be given for obsolete modes of speech, but what a venerable cast this alone often gives a writer. I omit the previous knowledge in ancient customs and manners, in grammar and construction; the knowledge of these is presupposed; to be caught tripping here is an ominous stumble; 'tis ignorance, which no guess-work, no divining faculty, however ingenious, can atone and commute for.

—John Upton,
Critical Observations on Shakespeare

Introduction

THERE IS perhaps no collection of English poetry more widely known and praised than Shakespeare's *Sonnets*, and certainly no collection of English poetry has been more often misused and misread. The chief obstacles to a liberal and intelligent reading of these Sonnets have been two sets of assumptions, whether conscious or unconscious—those about what poetry is or should be and those about the nature of the collection. As far as the first set of assumptions is concerned, we are generally better prepared than previous generations to do critical justice to the Sonnets; but since the body of expectations, of things taken for granted, about poetry varies from person to person as well as from generation to generation, there are still many readers whose concept of poetry prevents them from accepting these poems on their own merits. They want them to be more formal, more gnomic or didactic, more metaphysical—somehow different and "better."

Virtually unknown in the seventeenth century, the Sonnets were read by only a few men in the eighteenth, partly because of widespread prejudice against the sonnet as a trivial and artificial short poem. Readers of the Sonnets in the eighteenth century, like many in the nineteenth, apparently wished that the poems had been as John Benson described them in his edition of 1640, "Seren, cleere and eligantly plaine, . . . no intricate or

1

cloudy stuffe to puzzell intellect," instead of what they conceived them to be: the careless apprentice work of a famous writer, full of such unforgivable faults as far-fetched conceits, quibbles, or puns, obscurity, and lack of variety. The frustrated assumptions of this class of readers are implicit in an unfavorable comment written by Wordsworth before 1803:

> These sonnets beginning at CXXVII to his mis-
> tress, are worse than a puzzle-peg. They are abom-
> inably harsh, obscure, and worthless. The others
> are for the most part much better, have many fine
> lines very fine lines and passages. They are also in
> many places warm with passion. Their chief faults
> —and heavy ones they are—are sameness, tedious-
> ness, quaintness, and elaborate obscurity.[1]

Other readers of the nineteenth century, overwhelmed by what Dyce called their "transcendent beauty," extravagantly praised the Sonnets for their verbal melody, imagination, intensity of feeling, and the variety and keen observation of their imagery.[2] Like the readers of every generation, they were willing to praise, but only on their own terms; and the comments of nineteenth-century editors and critics on individual Sonnets reveal a general tendency, which has by no means vanished, to make Shakespeare's meaning as simple, as dull and flat, as possible. We at least have the advantage of be-lieving that all fluid or nontechnical discourse has mul-tiplicity of meaning; that ambiguity is not a fault in language but an inevitable consequence of its powers and "the indispensable means of most of our most im-portant utterances—especially in Poetry and Religion."[3] Hence it is far easier for us to perceive not only the melody, intensity, and variety of the Sonnets but also how complex, agile, and subtle Shakespeare's use of language in them often is.

The nineteenth century not only bequeathed to us its enthusiasm for the Sonnets, but that age of the historical method and modern or scientific scholarship also left us

2

the greatest obstacles to reading these poems for themselves—a confused set of views about the nature of the
collection and its relation to Shakespeare's life. They
are chiefly embodied in a mountain of books and articles
speculating on the identities of persons in or connected
with the Sonnets (e.g., Master W. H., the Fair Friend,
the Dark Lady) and rearranging the Sonnets to produce
a "better" or "right" order. Although we readily reject
the crudest of these conceptions and the conclusions
based upon them, we are all inclined to accept some of
the more insidious ones, which still confront us in almost every general introduction to the Sonnets. Yet
those which concern the order and interrelations of the
Sonnets should be carefully weighed by every critical
reader, for they affect the interpretation of individual
poems.

The order in which Shakespeare's Sonnets were first
printed in the Quarto of 1609 apparently satisfied very
few men, and thus there arose the great international
game of rearranging them. This is a game with a rich
past and a frightening future for two simple reasons: the
number of possible permutations and combinations of
154 poems is virtually infinite, and each player makes
his own rules, the theories and speculations on which
he bases his rearrangement. Since the list of players includes some intelligent and competent readers among
the eccentrics and fanatics, it is a mistake to suppose
that the rearranging game can provide nothing but
warning examples for critics and illustrations of the
vanity of human wishes. However misguided they may
be, the best of the rearrangers have carefully considered
the interrelations of all the Sonnets, and sometimes they
remind the reader of illuminating relationships which
he had overlooked.

In the absence of any external evidence which would
allow one to determine whether the arrangement of
Sonnets in the Quarto of 1609 is the work of Shakespeare, or Thomas Thorpe, or Master W. H., or X, most

3

editors have accepted the order of the Quarto. This is an order which deserves serious consideration, if only because no better one has ever been proposed. Indeed, all the rearrangers of the Sonnets have overlooked a few elementary facts which make their undertaking irrelevant and futile, namely, the nature of the Elizabethan sonnet "sequence" and the order of poems in Elizabethan sequences published *with* the author's consent. If one compares Shakespeare's Sonnets with such a typical collection as Spenser's *Amoretti* (1595), one finds that, although Shakespeare's sequence has more variety and more poems and addresses more than one person, it is no more incoherent, disorganized, or haphazard than the collection of sonnets arranged by Spenser. The fact is, the average Elizabethan sonnet sequence cannot be called a sequence in any strict sense of the word, and, although one person is usually addressed throughout, it is not organized upon any discernible internal principle.[4] Like the famous and seminal sonnet collection of Petrarch, which he appropriately called "fragments" and "scattered rimes,"[5] the Elizabethan sequence is essentially a collection of separate poems which tend to form small groups organized upon various principles.[6] It is an art *form* only by convention and not by virtue of a general principle of organization.

Most critics who disdain to impose a certain order and homogeneity upon Shakespeare's Sonnets by rearranging them do not hesitate to impose order by subscribing to the almost universal assumption that the collection consists of two groups of poems, a long series addressed to the Fair Youth (Sonnets 1–126) followed by a shorter series concerned with the Dark Lady (Sonnets 127–154).[7] Allowing for the crude and casual way in which we usually talk about poetry, there is perhaps something to be said for this traditional division of the Sonnets as a superficial method of indicating some obvious differences between the bulk of them and the last twenty-eight. For example, only in Sonnets 1–126 does one find the great abstractions of Time, Nature, and Fortune, discussions of the poet's muse, and claims that his poetry can confer immortality; and there is nothing to indicate that a woman is addressed anywhere in Sonnets 1–126, or a man in Sonnets 127–154. Yet whatever may be said for the convenience of this traditional grouping, there is far more that must be said against it. In the first place, it often rests on the misconception that each of the two groups is in some sense a sequence or series, that the collection as a whole is a work of art with some kind of continuity and form. The typical believer in the myth of two groups assumes that there is more uniformity in the Sonnets than in fact exists, and he often assumes that a narrative or story is present.[8] There is no more narrative in Shakespeare's than in Petrarch's collection;[9] what passes for a story can be extracted only by a mixture of fanciful speculation and reckless abstraction, that is to say, only by ignoring the poems as poems. The myth of two groups not only ignores the variety of the Sonnets, the integrity of the individual poem, and the nature of the Elizabethan sonnet sequence, but it also ignores the fact that the sex of the person addressed is *in no way* indicated or suggested in half of Sonnets 1–126, and that it is impossible to determine whether or not only one man is addressed in all the Sonnets containing references to males.

To condemn the various attempts which have been and are still being made to violate the nature of the collection and the integrity of the individual poem by imposing a false order on the Sonnets is not to deny that there are many significant relationships among them. It has long been evident that relations among contiguous Sonnets result in a few relatively large groups of poems and many small ones and that certain Sonnets which are separated from each other are also related. Many of the connections, and especially those between successive Sonnets, are intentional (Sonnets 5 and 6); others, especially those between widely separated poems, are perhaps unintentional (Sonnets 4 and 94, 20 and 53). Some of the connections are close and obvious (Sonnets 5 and 6, 50 and 51, 113 and 114), others, not as close or as obvious (Sonnets 4 and 94, 68 and 69). Perhaps none of the major relationships is without significance for the meaning of the participating Sonnets, but occasionally, as in the case of the similar Sonnets 57 and 58, which may be regarded as variations on a theme, the connection seems to have little or no effect on the general interpretation of either poem. But both juxtaposed and separated Sonnets often serve as a gloss for one another (Sonnets 20 and 53, 53 and 54, 93 and 94), and almost a necessary condition for the intelligent reading of certain Sonnets is an understanding of what others they are related to and how they are related. A sound knowledge of the major relationships among the Sonnets enables the reader to discover relevant contexts which may make adequate interpretation of a Sonnet or part of a Sonnet possible or easier or even more difficult (temporarily), but in virtually all cases these contexts are the basis of fuller understanding. For all interpretation, whether it is that ordinary commerce with things and events which we call sense perception or that special attention to special objects which we call criticism, is essentially a comparison of contexts. In the chapters which follow I shall attempt to support my remarks on the significance of these relationships by discussing some striking examples.

1

The Unmoved Movers:
SONNET 94 AND THE CONTEXTS
OF INTERPRETATION

And therefore as that water which is always standing and
never runneth must needs be noisome and infectious, so
that man which is never moved in mind can never be either
good to himself or profitable to others. But have them [pas-
sions] we must and use them we may, and that abundantly,
in honest wise.
—Thomas Rogers, *A Philosophical Discourse Entitled,*
The Anatomy of the Mind

THE FIRST SEVENTEEN (or nineteen) Sonnets are generally said to constitute a group [1] in which a handsome
young man is urged to marry and to win immortality
through his children. This group, perhaps the largest
of the whole collection, is rather loosely organized as
compared to the three sets of closely related poems
which it contains (Sonnets 5 and 6; 9 and 10; 12, 15,
and 16). The common principle of Sonnets 1–17 seems
to be the poet's avowed intention: to urge the youth to
continue his life and beauty through children. The first
Sonnet, "From fairest creatures we desire increase," ex-
emplifies both the stated common purpose of the group
and its frequent mixture of praise for the youth's beauty
with blame for his failure to use his beauty through marriage. Here in lines 5–8 he is charged with a Narcissus-
like self-love or self-containment by which he makes "a

7

famine where abundance lies" or (in more typical imagery) makes "waste in niggarding" (1. 12). The full implications of this last phrase and the doctrine underlying it are made clear in Sonnet 4, which I propose to use as a natural introduction to the interpretation of the great Sonnet 94, "They that have pow'r to hurt and will do none."

Sonnet 4 is a doctrinal poem embodying in a series of questions and statements what since medieval times was conceived to be the lesson of the Parable of the Talents—the wise use of the gifts of God or Nature.

> Unthrifty loveliness, why dost thou spend
> Upon thyself thy beauty's legacy?
> Nature's bequest gives nothing, but doth
>   lend,
> 4   And, being frank, she lends to those are free.
> Then, beauteous niggard, why dost thou
>   abuse
> The bounteous largess given thee to give?
> Profitless usurer, why dost thou use
> 8   So great a sum of sums, yet canst not live?
> For, having traffic with thyself alone,
> Thou of thyself thy sweet self dost deceive.
> Then how, when Nature calls thee to be
>   gone,
> 12 What acceptáble audit canst thou leave?
> Thy unused beauty must be tombed
>   with thee,
> Which, uséd, lives th' executor to be.[2]

"Thy beauty's legacy" in line 2 is equivalent to the legacy of your beauty, "legacy" having the senses something handed down from an ancestor (his beauty handed down from his parents) and a gift by will (his beauty as Nature's bequest). The imagery of the first three and the last four lines of the poem is highly appropriate because the parent-child relationship is generally the focus of testamentary affairs, and the imagery of financial transactions in lines 4–10 grows easily out

8

of the imagery of the opening through the various senses of lending. The third and fourth lines contain the central proposition: Nature gives nothing outright but only lends; grants the temporary possession and use of excellences of mind and body, expecting that what is lent or its equivalent will be returned; makes a loan and hence expects repayment with interest.[3] Since she is generous and liberal herself, Nature lends her gifts to those who are the same. These lines closely resemble the last five lines of a passage in *Measure for Measure* (I.i. 29–40), a passage which also derives its doctrine from the Parable of the Talents (Matt. 25:14–30):

> Thyself and thy belongings
> Are not thine own so proper, as to waste
> Thyself upon thy virtues, they on thee.
> Heaven doth with us as we with torches do,
> Not light them for themselves; for if our
>   virtues
> Did not go forth of us, 'twere all alike
> As if we had them not. Spirits are not finely
>   touch'd
> But to fine issues, nor Nature never lends
> The smallest scruple of her excellence,
> But, like a thrifty goddess, she determines
> Herself the glory of a creditor,
> Both thanks and use.[4]

The question of lines 5–6 of the sonnet,[5] emphasizing the contrast between the youth's miserliness and Nature's munificence, is restated by lines 7–8 in terms of usury, which suggests the enrichment desired by the world and Nature.[6] "Use" in line 7 carries three or four different meanings, all of which should be taken seriously. Perhaps the senses which accuse the youth of waste and negligence—use up, consume; have at one's disposal, have the use of—are what the speaker insists upon, and yet others—make use of, employ; lend at interest, invest—are required by the imagery. "Canst not live" in line 8 is less ambiguous; it signifies both cannot

9

make a living (as a usurer) and cannot continue in life, cannot escape oblivion (without a child). "Live" and "use" are good examples of something that Shakespeare, unlike many of his editors, was well aware of and frequently exploited, namely, that a word may be both literal and metaphorical at the same time.

To the extent that Sonnet 4 is based on the doctrine of good stewardship or the lesson of the Parable of the Talents, it is related to Sonnet 94; but it is obvious that in most respects these poems hardly could be more different. Although Sonnet 94 may be related to various contexts in various ways, like some of the finest poems in the collection it also seems to stand alone; for like Sonnets 66, 121, 125, and 129, it is timeless, general, and unique. In Sonnet 4 the doctrine is adjusted to the "birth in beauty" motif of the opening group, but it is also quite directly stated in brief and general form. In the case of the rich, complex, and subtle Sonnet 94 the doctrine enters only indirectly into the sense of the poem (what is being said), and yet it exerts considerable control over the way it is said, for the Parable provides the imagery of the second quatrain and a traditional basis for its irony:

> They that have pow'r to hurt and will do
>   none,
> That do not do the thing they most do show,
> Who, moving others, are themselves as
>   stone,
> 4 Unmovèd, cold, and to temptation slow—
> They rightly do inherit heaven's graces
> And husband nature's riches from expense;
> They are the lords and owners of their faces,
> 8 Others but stewards of their excellence.
> The summer's flow'r is to the summer sweet,
> Though to itself it only live and die;
> But if that flow'r with base infection meet,
> 12 The basest weed outbraves his dignity:

10

For sweetest things turn sourest by their
  deeds;
Lilies that fester smell far worse than
  weeds.

If a reader were quite ignorant of all the most relevant contexts of interpretation, he might well miss the
drift of the Sonnet's octave, although the charge of feeling, the emotional attitude, and thus the irony of these
lines seem unmistakable. However, the typical inter-
preter of this Sonnet is familiar with the Sonnets, *Measure for Measure,* and the Bible, and yet he distorts the
poem seriously. There is no simple explanation for this
curious state of affairs, but a brief comparison of some
typical interpretations of Sonnet 94 should prove in-
structive, helping us to discover some of the poem's
basic difficulties and hence some of the chief opportu-
nities for misinterpretation.

To begin with the most obvious oversimplification of
the Sonnet, consider this statement of the theme of Sonnets 94–96 by the distinguished scholar J. Q. Adams:
"the friend has fallen into a life of gross sensuality, and
the poet finds it necessary to rebuke him in the strongest language." [7] By strongest language he means the last
four lines of Sonnet 94, which he quotes at the end of
his comment. It is ironic that Mr. Adams should be
aware of the relevance of the Parable of the Talents to
Sonnet 4 [8] and utterly fail to perceive its bearing on this
poem; but perhaps it would be fairer to say that he rejects it instead of overlooking it, for interpretation consists of rejecting some contexts and readings while accepting others, of deciding what a poem does not mean
as well as what it does. In this case Mr. Adams has
focused his attention on the more immediate yet less
relevant context provided by Sonnet 95, "How sweet
and lovely dost thou make the shame," with its references to sins, vices, and sexual sport.

Although in some respects it is far more specific and

11

careful, John Crowe Ransom's paraphrase of Sonnet 94 shares some of the weaknesses of the preceding comment. Attempting to relate the poem's large and sententious thought-units to what he calls the "facts of the story" (of Shakespeare, the Fair Youth, and the Dark Lady), he depends upon a similar context, with the result that he too views the poem as simply a warning against sexual indulgence:

> You have your own free will, to be unchaste or not, and your beauty exposes you to the temptation of women. But consider yourself as sole inheritor from heaven of this beauty, and expected to keep it to yourself; those who share their beauty in sex must regard themselves as but its stewards. There is no reproach upon the flower for being self-contained. But infected flowers smell to heaven.[9]

The first sentence of this paraphrase suggests that Mr. Ransom reads the poem in the light of Sonnet 41, "Those pretty wrongs that liberty commits," one of three Sonnets (40–42) addressed to a handsome young friend who has betrayed the poet by having sexual relations with his mistress. Ransom's subsequent remarks make it clear that such is the case:

> The personal reference under this paraphrase would lie in Shakespeare's urging W. H. to have no lovers, especially among women. The terms of the argument we have met with before, though the argument is now reversed; see IV, V, VI, X, XVII, and XX, for instance. The sonnets which open the sequence urge the patron repeatedly to marry, and claim that indeed he is but the steward of his beauty. But that was before Shakespeare's own dark lady seduced the patron.[10]

With Sonnet 41 as a controlling context, "temptation" (l. 4) inevitably becomes the temptation of women, and "faces" (l. 7), which is equated with "heaven's graces" (l. 5) and "nature's riches" (l. 6), becomes beauty. Both of these readings obviously limit the scope of the poem.

12

Since the sestet is a kind of parable designed to reinforce the meaning of the octave, the interpretation of the octave usually determines that of the sestet, as it does in this paraphrase. However, here too there is reason to believe that all is not as clear and simple as Mr. Ransom makes it.

The interpretation of Edward Dowden is more detailed than Mr. Ransom's and in some respects more satisfactory; yet, although he was the first critic to note the relevance of *Measure for Measure* (I.i.36 ff.) to Sonnet 4, he ignores its present relevance and thus like the others he misses the irony of Sonnet 94's second quatrain.

In xciii. Shakespere has described his friend as able to show a sweet face while harbouring false thoughts; the subject is enlarged on in the present sonnet. They who can hold their passions in check, who can refuse to wrath its outbreak, who can seem loving yet keep a cool heart, who move passion in others, yet are cold and unmoved themselves—they rightly inherit from heaven large gifts, for they husband them; whereas passionate intemperate natures squander their endowments; those who can assume this or that semblance as they see reason are the masters and owners of their faces; others have no property in such excellences as they possess, but hold them for the advantage of the prudent self-contained persons. True, these self-contained persons may seem to lack generosity; but then, without making voluntary gifts, they give inevitably, even as the summer's flower is sweet to the summer, though it live and die only to itself. Yet let such an one beware of corruption, which makes odious the sweetest flowers.[11]

This paraphrase has two commendable features: it suggests that Shakespeare's attitude toward the "lords and owners of their faces" is not one of pure admiration, and it indicates the value of the immediate context of

Sonnet 93 as a partial gloss on the octave of Sonnet 94. (Indeed, all three commentaries may serve to remind the critic that it is always advisable to study carefully several Sonnets preceding and following the one he wishes to interpret.) One of the more interesting poems in the collection, Sonnet 93 emphasizes the contrast between the looks or face that presents the appearance of love and the heart or thoughts that (may) bear no love; this potential contrast between attractive appearance and ugly reality is summarized in the couplet in terms which convey the speaker's distaste:

> So shall I live, supposing thou art true,
> Like a deceivèd husband; so love's face
> May still seem love to me, though altered
>   new—
> 4 Thy looks with me, thy heart in other place.
> For there can live no hatred in thine eye;
> Therefore in that I cannot know thy change.
> In many's looks the false heart's history
> 8 Is writ in moods and frowns and wrinkles
>   strange;
> But heaven in thy creation did decree
> That in thy face sweet love should ever dwell;
> Whate'er thy thoughts or thy heart's work-
>   ings be,
> 12 Thy looks should nothing thence but sweet-
>   ness tell.
> How like Eve's apple doth thy beauty
>   grow
> If thy sweet virtue answer not thy show! [12]

Dowden quite rightly uses the sense of Sonnet 93 as a guide to some of the more specific implications of the generalizations in the octave of Sonnet 94. He points out that one way in which the unmoved movers "do not do the thing they most do show" is that they appear to love but do not,[13] and he regards the ambiguous seventh line as referring to their complete self-possession, a view which is supported by lines 7–12 of Sonnet 93 as well as by the first quatrain of Sonnet 94. But, although he uses one aspect of Sonnet 93's meaning, the sense, to help him gloss these lines, he rejects an equally important aspect—its charge of feeling, which is not only carried over into Sonnet 94 (with certain differences) but also in some respects greatly intensified. Dowden is aware that Shakespeare does not regard the unmoved movers with complete approval—note his comment, "these self-contained persons may seem to lack generosity"—but like Adams and Ransom he takes "rightly" (l. 5) at its face value and accepts the lords and owners as praiseworthy examples, though of temperance and self-control rather than mere chastity.

What the critical labors of these literalists illustrate is that how one reads this Sonnet is largely a matter of what contexts are brought to bear on it. The selection of these contexts may, in turn, depend upon general assumptions, conscious and unconscious, about the order and nature of the collection, as the comments of Ransom and Dowden indicate. It is no accident that Dowden reads the poem in the light of Sonnet 93, for he is "convinced . . . that the Sonnets stand in the right order, and that sonnet is connected with sonnet in more instances than have been observed." [14] As a result, the notes in his edition confirm Beeching's remark that he "shows infinite ingenuity in connecting every sonnet with its predecessor." In any case, it is natural that the immediate context of Sonnet 94, the paired Sonnets 92 and 93, 95 and 96, should receive the most attention and exert the greatest influence upon interpretation. But, as I hope to make clear, the Sonnet is related to these pairs in different ways, and its relationship with Sonnets 95 and 96 is less important and illuminating. The more closely connected Sonnet 93 can provide the basis for an adequate reading of Sonnet 94, and yet it did not prevent Dowden and others from distorting the second quatrain. That is where the first seventeen Sonnets, especially Sonnet 4, *Measure for Measure,* and the

Parable of the Talents can be genuinely useful—by reinforcing or guiding our perception of the speaker's feeling and tone and thus preventing us from falsifying the entire poem.

II

I shall begin my attempt to sketch a general interpretation of Sonnet 94 with a brief discussion of its place in a provisional group comprising Sonnets 87–96. Within this group Sonnets 87–93 are held together by what might be called their general subject—as opposed to the particular subject of each Sonnet—the poet's fear of losing the love of the male (or female) friend he addresses.[15] Sonnet 87, "Farewell! thou art too dear for my possessing," is a kind of resigned and ironic introduction to the group.[16] The parallel or companion Sonnets 88 and 89 dwell on the poet's willingness to fight against himself, to exaggerate his faults for his friend's sake. Both of them indicate that the poet loves far more than he is loved in return and that his love is humble and unselfish. To put it in terms of major traditions, it is a love that has in it far more of *agapé* (a stream of givings) than of *eros* (a stream of gettings).[17]

> For, bending all my loving thoughts on thee,
> The injuries that to myself I do,
> Doing thee vantage, double-vantage me.
> Such is my love, to thee I so belong,
> That for thy right myself will bear all
> wrong.   (Sonnet 88, ll. 10–14)

Sonnet 90, "Then hate me when thou wilt . . . ," picks up "hate," the last word of Sonnet 89, "Say that thou didst forsake me for some fault," and invites the friend to hate him now, if ever, while he is tasting fortune's "spite." In Sonnet 91, "Some glory in their birth . . . ," after enumerating things which others glory in, Shakespeare asserts that to him his friend's love is better than all of them; he is "wretched in this alone, that thou mayst take / All this away and me most wretched make." The sense of this couplet is continued by opposition in Sonnet 92, "But do thy worst to steal thyself away": as long as he lives he will have his friend, for his very life depends upon the friend's love. However, the last line, "Thou mayst be false, and yet I know it not," introduces a new note which is continued and expanded in Sonnet 93.

Sonnets 95 and 96 clearly belong together because of their general subject, the remarkable ability of the friend to remain attractive despite obvious vices. Ostensibly emphasizing his friend's surface attractiveness, in Sonnet 95 the poet sets forth the disparity between the beautiful appearance and the ugly reality and concludes with a warning that one cannot sin with impunity. Sonnet 96, "Some say thy fault is youth, some wantonness," first comments on his friend's talent for making faults graces and translating errors to truths, and then urges the friend not to use the strength of all his "state" to lead others astray.

This brings us to the question of the relation of Sonnet 94 to the subgroups consisting of Sonnets 87–93 and 95–96. Without minimizing its individuality and scope, I suggest that Sonnet 94 is the natural bridge between them, with its octave looking back to Sonnets 87–93 and its sestet looking forward to Sonnets 95–96. In Sonnet 87 Shakespeare takes it for granted that he has lost his superior friend; then for a few poems the loss becomes a possibility which has not yet been realized. As we approach Sonnet 94 the fear of loss seems to grow stronger, even though its potentiality is specified: "Thou *mayst* be false, and yet I know it not," "How like Eve's apple doth thy beauty grow / *If* thy sweet virtue answer not thy show." But the use of "mayst" in Sonnet 92 and "if" in 93 is probably only a concession to love, a way of temporarily refusing to face the facts of the situation; for those facts are faced squarely and the possible loss treated as an actuality in the octave of Sonnet 94. Here with irony, ambivalence, and ambiguity Shakespeare addresses and describes his superior friend, whose personal worth and riches he had extolled (somewhat ironically) in Sonnet 87, as an example of the Aristotelian self-sufficient man whose motto might be, "What need of friends, when Heaven bestows the good?" [18]

> They that have pow'r to hurt and will do
> none,
> That do not do the thing they most do show,
> Who, moving others, are themselves as stone,
> Unmovèd, cold, and to temptation slow—
> They rightly do inherit heaven's graces
> And husband nature's riches from expense;
> They are the lords and owners of their faces,
> Others but stewards of their excellence.

Then in the sestet he presents a parable warning of the dangers to which such natures are open, the corruption which may result when they lose their self-sufficiency.[19] In the words of the old proverb, "the corruption of the best is worst," as the case of Angelo in *Measure for Measure* illustrates.[20]

> The summer's flow'r is to the summer sweet,
> Though to itself it only live and die;
> But *if* that flow'r with base infection meet,
> The basest weed outbraves his dignity:
> For sweetest things turn sourest by their
> deeds;
> Lilies that fester smell far worse than
> weeds.

This potential corruption of excellence has become actual in Sonnet 95:

> How sweet and lovely dost thou make the
> shame
> Which, like a canker in the fragrant rose,
> Doth spot the beauty of thy budding name!
> 4 O, in what sweets dost thou thy sins enclose!
> That tongue that tells the story of thy days
> (Making lascivious comments on thy sport)
> Cannot dispraise but in a kind of praise:

8　Naming thy name blesses an ill report.
　　O, what a mansion have those vices got
　　Which for their habitation chose out thee,
　　Where beauty's veil doth cover every blot
12　And all things turns to fair that eyes can see!
　　　　Take heed, dear heart, of this large privi-
　　　　　lege;
　　　　The hardest knife ill used doth lose his
　　　　　edge.

Let me now introduce a schema which will not only summarize my argument on the place of Sonnet 94 in its group, but also make it clear why I object to interpretation of its octave in terms of Sonnets 95 and 96:

Appearance vs. Reality:　　87–91

looks　　*false heart*　　92 *mayst*　Potential loss of friend's love
show　　*virtue*　　　　93 *if*　　　increasingly feared

show　　*do not do*
(What need of friends when　94 Octave—actual loss of friend's love:
heaven provides *graces*?)　　　*as stone, unmoved, cold*　　Self-
　　　　　　　　　　　　　　　　　　sufficient
　　　　　　　　　　　　　　　　　　people
(The good things of life　94 Sestet—potential corruption of　(including
corrupt and distract the　　friend (*if*); flower as emblem　friend)
soul: *lilies that fester*)　　or symbol: *summer's flower,*
　　　　　　　　　　　　　　lilies that fester

veil　　*blot*　　　　95 flower as
(*canker in the fragrant rose*)　image·　　actual corruption
graces　　*faults*　　96　　　of friend: *sport*

The generality of Sonnet 94 is in a sense a defense or protective disguise adopted by love, a way of saying to the friend, "You are one of a class (of men and women); there are others like you"; yet it is predominantly a transparent device for directing an accusation: "Some people I know are cold and selfish." Shakespeare has mixed feelings about the friend as unmoved mover, is simultaneously attracted and repelled. The positive component of this ambivalence is the love or admiration which the friend's worth still elicits; the negative component is more complex. It consists of dislike of the friend's coldness, deriving from a desire for some return for love given, since no love can be pure *agapé* or giving; dislike of the simulation emphasized in Sonnet 93 and here in the first quatrain; and perhaps dislike of the corruption to which the friend's advantages expose him.

To speak of the ambivalence of the octave of Sonnet 94 is to speak of its irony, for from the psychological point of view irony "is the bringing in of the opposite, the complementary impulses." [21] However, it is also a figure of rhetoric, a linguistic maneuver that is a kind of dissimulation, as its etymology signifies; so that here one finds Shakespeare using appearance versus reality in a linguistic device to criticize appearance versus reality in human behavior. Beneath the surface of commendation or approval of unmoved movers glows an accumulation of bitterness. This bitterness begins to emerge in the ambiguous and harshly objective description of the first quatrain. For most readers, however, it is submerged and lost in the second quatrain, where the status of unmoved movers as lords and owners is commented on, ostensibly from their own point of view or some equally favorable one. But the imagery should make the feeling and tone of these lines clear, or at least, by bringing to bear the Parable of the Talents and some of the early Sonnets, cast strong doubt on the extent to which the sense is to be taken literally.

20

selves like stone—impassive, cold, and highly resistant to attraction by anything or anyone, including those whom they affect. Among the personal relationships to which they are so resistant may be those of friendship and sex; they make others love them as friends or sexual partners but remain quite unaffected themselves. "To temptation slow," which Schmidt regards as equivalent to "slowly tempted," [26] makes a point in favor of the unmoved movers as a reference to enticement to sin or evil; and yet as a reference to morally neutral attraction, it also scores a point against them. As Thomas Rogers remarked in A Philosophical Discourse (1576), "that man which is never moved in mind can never be either good to himself or profitable to others." [27]

> They rightly do inherit heaven's graces
> And husband nature's riches from expense

It is right and fitting that they should have the gifts of God and nature, and they possess and enjoy them in the right way, saving them from expenditure, waste, and loss. The heavily ironic "rightly" has two obvious senses, and "heaven's graces," which is synonymous with "nature's riches," refers to pleasing qualities, excellences of body *and* mind.[28] "Husband" (to administer as a good steward, to manage thriftily and prudently; to make the most of, economize; to save) raises the question of the difference between conserving and hoarding, the question of what constitutes good stewardship, something about which lords and owners know nothing.

> They are the lords and owners of their faces

They are the only ones who possess their talents or riches; they have complete mastery of their faces, of their appearance, so that one can never tell anything about their real feelings or thoughts. "Faces" is both a deliberate reminder of the deceitful looks and face of Sonnet 93 [29] and, as the equivalent of physical beauty, a representative of *all* their excellences. Of course it is absurd to think of them as the actual lords and owners of their gifts, for they are clearly *heaven's* graces and nature's riches. Paul makes this clear (I Cor. 6:19-20), and Augustine and Calvin remind us, "Nothing is ours, but sin."

Others but stewards of their excellence

In marked contrast to the lords and owners are those who are merely the administrators and dispensers of their own gifts and those who are only the servants of the lords and owners' good qualities. "But stewards" is clearly ironic; "their" may refer to lords and owners as well as to stewards.[30] The inhumanly cold and selfish unmoved movers are being compared unfavorably with (a) those who are equally gifted but warm and generous, and (b) those (like the speaker) who are their servants or slaves because they are moved by them.[31] The basic contrast is between hoarders and keepers, users and givers. Lords and owners have so much that they easily could afford to give of their talents, to use and develop their powers, but instead they save them like the unprofitable servant who hid his talent and was cast into darkness. They forget that, though they may be lords and superior to their stewards, like all men they are themselves only stewards to the Lord: [32]

stewards: lords and owners::lords and owners:the
Lord (Heaven, Nature)
speaker:friend::friend:Heaven, Nature

Those who administer nature's riches must avoid the extremes of squandering or hoarding them if they are to be good stewards. Unmoved movers are in no danger of erring through wanton prodigality, but they do make waste in niggarding and thus are to be condemned as bad stewards; for "they that suppresse the giftes of God, and live in idlenes, are without all excuse."[33]

Since there are sharp and obvious differences between octave and sestet, the Sonnet provides a classic example of the so-called Petrarchan break. The sestet consists of a parable for unmoved movers, in which they are represented by the symbol or emblem of the summer's flower. One may regard the third quatrain as the body of the parable and the sententious summarizing couplet as its moral or conclusion.

> *The summer's flow'r is to the summer sweet,*
> *Though to itself it only live and die*

The flower is pleasing and valuable to its environment, though it only lives and dies by and for itself; [34] comparatively isolated and independent, it still contributes something to the season just by being itself. "Summer" is hard to pin down because there are numerous possibilities: nature, heaven, society, a generation, acquaintances (especially the speaker), and so on. "Sweet" has a whole range of relevant meanings, including having a pleasant odor, generally pleasing, wholesome, and dearly prized. Evidently the summer's flower is like the unmoved mover in at least two respects: it *does* nothing, that is, it merely exists and is effortlessly attractive, and it is virtually self-contained. Compare "A Lover's Complaint," lines 75–77:

> I might as yet have been a spreading flower,
> Fresh to myself, if I had self-applied
> Love to myself and to no love beside.

Compare also these remarks by Jeremy Taylor in his "Discourse of . . . Friendship": ". . . I will not weigh the gayest flowers, or the wings of butterflies, against wheat; but when I am to choose wheat, I may take that which looks the brightest. I had rather see thyme and roses, marjoram and July-flowers, that are fair, sweet, and medicinal, than the prettiest tulips, that are good for nothing." [35]

The next two lines introduce another similarity, an ominous one which it is the parable's chief purpose to make vivid.

> *But if that flow'r with base infection meet,*
> *The basest weed outbraves his dignity*

But *if* that pleasing and valuable flower comes into contact with or experiences disease or contamination, the most worthless weed surpasses it in beauty and value. Both flower and unmoved mover are defenseless, in some respects most open to debasement and corruption. "Meet with" has meanings ranging from "come into contact, association, or junction with," to "encounter, experience" (a certain fortune or destiny); the first suggests they are quite susceptible to infection,[36] the second, that they are merely unfortunate. "Base infection" signifies moral contamination, and, since Shakespeare occasionally uses "infect" in the sense of "to affect" and "infection" for "affection," it may also be glossed as base affection: what corrupts the normally unmoved mover is a base desire that is suddenly experienced—like Angelo's lust for Isabella in *Measure for Measure* (II.ii. 162–187).

> *For sweetest things turn sourest by their deeds;*
> *Lilies that fester smell far worse than weeds*

For the most attractive and valuable creatures can become the most contemptible and evil through their actions; lilies that rot smell far worse than healthy foul-smelling weeds. As the sweet odor of a flower constitutes its virtue, its excellence and essence (Sonnet 54), so the moral wholesomeness of man constitutes his essential excellence; without that inner sweetness he is only a rank show (Sonnet 69) or a festered lily.[37] Unmoved movers in their natural gifts, their cold beauty, purity, and conspicuousness are like healthy lilies; [38] when they become corrupt, like rotten lilies they will have the foulest odor.[39]

There is obviously much more to be said about such a rich poem, one which no doubt I have simplified and distorted to some extent. But any interpretation is inevitably inadequate in comparison to the poem as concretely experienced by a good reader, if only because of the demands of clarity and orderliness of exposition and the necessary selectivity of emphasis. On this last point I must say that my emphasis on the Parable is for the sake of elucidating the Sonnet's feeling and tone and should not be taken as an indication that I view the poem as a piece of pious moralizing or didacticism. Doubtless the general moral issues are important, but they are probably raised in the interests of "personal" feeling, as a means of buttressing the poet's private opinion.[40]

2

The Canker in the Rose:
SONNETS 69 AND 70, 53 AND 54

I say that beauty cometh of God and is like a circle, the goodness whereof is the center. And therefore, as there can be no circle without a center, no more can beauty be without goodness.
Sir Thomas Hoby, *The Courtier of Count Baldessar Castilio*

And is not the fairest sight of all, . . . for him who has eyes to see it, the combination in the same person of good character and good looks to match them, each bearing the same stamp?

Plato, *The Republic*

Those who read me know my conviction that the world, the temporal world, rests on a few very simple ideas: so simple that they must be as old as the hills. It rests, notably, among others, on the idea of Fidelity.

Joseph Conrad, *A Personal Record*

THERE ARE, of course, many kinds and degrees of ambiguity, as Empson pointed out some years ago.[1] In the case of Sonnet 94, for example, to make a crude but convenient distinction, there is an external as well as internal ambiguity, since its relation to adjoining Sonnets is not immediately clear. Thus different readers have selected different Sonnets to serve as the contexts controlling its interpretation. I now wish to consider two more cases of external ambiguity, one fairly simple, the other more subtle and complex. Here Sonnets which in isolation or in a neutral context would probably admit of only one general kind of reading, whatever the variations in the handling of ambiguous details, may in fact be interpreted in at least two different ways because of the influence of contiguous and noncontiguous Sonnets. These interpretations, like those of Sonnet 94, are not equally acceptable: one seems more defensible and probable than another, for in these matters there can be no certainty.

Taken by itself, Sonnet 69 must, I think, strike the reader as a fairly simple poem requiring little critical comment, except perhaps for its last three lines. Throughout the quatrains the speaker appears to present impartially the world's view of the disparity between his friend's outward beauty and inward corruption; in the couplet he states the basis of this marked discrepancy. There is, in short, plainly a certain degree of moral condemnation expressed:

> Those parts of thee that the world's eye doth view
> Want nothing that the thought of hearts can mend.
> All tongues (the voice of souls) give thee that due,
> 4 Utt'ring bare truth, even so as foes commend.
> Thy outward thus with outward praise is crowned;
> But those same tongues that give thee so thine own
> In other accents do this praise confound
> 8 By seeing farther than the eye hath shown.
> They look into the beauty of thy mind,
> And that in guess they measure by thy deeds;
> Then, churls, their thoughts (although their eyes were kind)
> 12 To thy fair flower add the rank smell of weeds;

But why thy odor matcheth not thy show,
The soil is this, that thou dost common
        grow.

If this Sonnet stood alone, the critic's main job would
be to assess the *degree* of moral condemnation that it
conveys in itself. But since it is followed by a related
Sonnet which "seems to say that the common opinion
is slander," [2] the task must consist in evaluating Sonnet
70 also and deciding just how much emphasis or weight
it should carry.

That thou art blamed shall not be thy defect,
For slander's mark was ever yet the fair;
The ornament of beauty is suspect,
4   A crow that flies in heaven's sweetest air.
So thou be good, slander doth but approve
Thy worth the greater, being wooed of time;
For canker vice the sweetest buds doth love,
8   And thou present'st a pure unstainèd prime.
Thou hast passed by the ambush of young
        days,
Either not assailed, or victor being charged;
Yet this thy praise cannot be so thy praise
12 To tie up envy, evermore enlarged.
If some suspect of ill masked not thy show,
Then thou alone kingdoms of hearts
        shouldst owe.

Unfortunately, most editors and commentators, committed to the Fair Friend and Dark Lady grouping of
the Sonnets and to firm views on the order of the Quarto,
are hardly disposed to consider the relationship of these
two Sonnets in a purely critical light. As Alden puts it
in a note on Sonnet 70,

This sonnet has awakened discussion chiefly
through its apparent inconsistency with others
commonly taken as addressed to the same person.
Critics undertake interpretations naturally, according as they view the unity and continuity of the
Sonnets in general.[3]

It is precisely because they are so concerned with the Sonnets *in general* that this pair has proved a sharp thorn in their sides. However useful many of their comments on details may be, their diverting antics and evasive tactics in regard to the general issue are rather annoying. There is nothing to be gained by ignoring the problem entirely, as Wyndham does; [4] or by giving a superficial summary of each poem, as Dowden does:

> LXIX. From the thought of his friend's external beauty Shakespere turns to think of the beauty of his mind, and the popular report against it.

> LXX. Continues the subject of the last sonnet, and defends his friend from the suspicion and slander of the time.[5]

Nor can the problem be resolved by rearranging the Sonnets, in the manner of Baldensperger, Bray, and Walsh; [6] or by assuming two different friends:

> Sonnet 70 indubitably follows 69; but it is, on the surface . . . inconsistent with it. . . . Whether the explanation be that Shakespeare was hoping the best and giving precept in the form of praise, we cannot say; but the point to notice here is that as 69 and 70 cannot be separated, the inconsistency cannot be got rid of by the hypothesis of more friends than one.[7]

These remarks by Beeching indicate that he has faced the inconsistency squarely and suggest that his views may be worth attention. Indeed, "hoping the best and giving precept in the form of praise" is fairly acute as a passing comment on Sonnet 70, but in his comments on Sonnet 69 he unfortunately veers in the opposite direction, even though he still refuses to commit himself entirely:

> the ensuing sonnet seems to say that the common opinion is slander. But a line in 121.12, "By their rank thoughts my deeds must not be shown," implies that deeds are capable of various interpretations; and the impression we get from the sonnet is

31

that the poet believes (or tries to believe) his friend to be really good despite certain lapses. See 95.13.[8]

Despite the qualifications here, which are probably due as much to an uneasy critical conscience as to a commendable caution, Beeching is evidently playing the common and understandable game of reading Sonnet 69 in terms of 70, with a minimizing of the moral censure as the result. It is curious that in his note he should cite Sonnets 95 and 121, for despite its general subject Sonnet 121, " 'Tis better to be vile than vile esteemed," is not very relevant, and Sonnet 95 undermines his position. But whether he is trimming or only trying to be fair, the fact remains that his remarks on Sonnets 69 and 70 are as ambiguous as he conceives their relationship to be.

It would be pleasant to be able to say that one of the most recent discussions of these poems is an index of how far criticism of the Sonnets has traveled since Beeching's time; but, alas, though it is much fuller and far more sophisticated, J. W. Lever's commentary is just as unsatisfactory—for quite different reasons. He finds that Sonnet 69 "opens with a good deal of embarrassed hesitancy, and winds rather wordily to a point that is not made until the final couplet." I must confess that this embarrassed hesitancy quite escapes me, as well as the "Bottom-like absurdity of tongues that see too far" as a "measure of the Poet's awkwardness." One naturally takes "tongues" in the second quatrain as a simple and appropriate example of metonymy or synecdoche. Line 12 "is uncomfortably reminiscent of the Mistress in CXXXI, who was black in nothing save her deeds." Whatever value this reference to Sonnet 131 may have as a way of suggesting a *serious* disparity between physical appearance and moral reality is immediately offset by the use of "slander" in the next sentence: "The couplet instead of rebutting the slander merely adds a reproach." [9]

32

One would almost automatically assume that Lever regards Sonnet 69's estimate of the friend as a piece of slander because he follows the common practice of reading it in the light of Sonnet 70. However, the heart of his discussion of Sonnet 69, combined with his justifiable refusal to take 70 very seriously, indicates that in fact he reads it in terms of Sonnet 54, "O, how much more doth beauty beauteous seem":

> The Rose, it cannot be denied, has begun to grow wild, and is in course of degeneration to the common scentless canker-bloom. The blame is still chiefly laid upon the society he keeps, but the contact is more than incidental; he is rooted in the same soil. As usual, slander goes further than fact; not content that he has lost the odour and ornament of truth, it must associate him with the rank smell of weeds, Shakespeare's favorite image for the grosser sensualities of propagation. The very fact that the canker-rose should thus be confused with rank weeds shows how baseless was the attribution of sterility in LIV. Evidently the distinction between wild rose and wild garlic is not absolute: both have their roots in the common earth . . . ; so has the cultivated rose.[10]

Here Lever is apparently the victim of the order of his grouping, his conception of unity, and his efforts to unfold the "fragmentary story"; for in the group which he calls "The Friend's Fault" he puts Sonnet 54 just before 69 and 70, and, like his other groups, it is to be regarded as a unit.[11] Sonnet 54 deals with the difference between merely external beauty and beauty having the sweet odor of "truth" by means of the contrasted emblems of the "scentless canker-bloom" and the sweet rose. Thus in imagery and general subject it bears a general resemblance to Sonnet 69, among others, but this hardly justifies such a crude and explicit application of its emblems as one finds here. There is no fact in Sonnet 54 which might serve as a basis for determining whether or not there is slander in 69, and hence no basis for postulating a confusion of the canker-rose with rank weeds—if one is reading each poem properly.

I doubt that I am being grossly unfair to Lever, although it would be more charitable to assume that he derives the slander of 69 from 70 while choosing to discuss it in metaphors taken from 54, partly because he regards the rose as "one of the main structural images of the sequence." [12] But, apart from the obvious dangers of such a course, his discussion of Sonnet 70 makes it unlikely that I am misconstruing his use of contexts. For he opens his discussion with the statement that "having conceded that the slanders are not wholly baseless, the Poet is driven to employ some rather transparent casuistry"; and he concludes by noting that the Sonnet "ends with a return to casuistry. . . . The argument is entirely without conviction, and merely employs flattery to cover the Poet's retreat from the moral dilemmas into which he has been driven by the Friend's conduct." [13]

II

Sonnet 69 consists mainly of the poet's relatively impartial report of the world's view of his friend.[14]

> Those parts of thee that the world's eye doth
>   view
> Want nothing that the thought of hearts can
>   mend.
> All tongues (the voice of souls) give thee
>   that due,
> 4 Utt'ring bare truth, even so as foes commend.
> Thy outward thus with outward praise is
>   crowned;
> But those same tongues that give thee so
>   thine own
> In other accents do this praise confound
> 8 By seeing farther than the eye hath shown.
> They look into the beauty of thy mind,

And that in guess they measure by thy deeds;
Then, churls, their thoughts (although their
eyes were kind)
12   To thy fair flower add the rank smell of
weeds;
But why thy odor matcheth not thy show,
The soil is this, that thou dost common
grow.[15]

In the first quatrain he presents the favorable portion of the general opinion: everyone admits that his friend's physical beauty is perfect, lacking nothing that one might think of to improve it. In acknowledging this, people are only being just, uttering no more than the simple truth, commending just as enemies do—reluctantly and without any exaggeration. Thus his friend's external appearance is given the crown of public praise, or is crowned (victor or king) by overt praise (l. 5).[16] But, the poet goes on to say in the rest of the second quatrain, the same people who render this just praise destroy it in other language—the language of thoughts—by perceiving what lies beneath his friend's physical beauty. They inquire into the matter of his mind's beauty, of which they make a rough estimate from his deeds (ll. 9–10). Then, although their eyes had favored him, misers and low peasants that they are— "churls" is probably ironic—their thoughts disapprove of his moral defects: to the fair flower of his appearance they add the foul odor of common weeds (ll. 11–12). It only remains for the poet to support public opinion by speaking for himself in the couplet as he bluntly informs his friend of the reason for the disparity between his odor and show, namely, that he is becoming common.

In order to assess the degree of condemnation in this Sonnet, one must consider the implication of the pejoratives in lines 12–14 and the palliative context provided by the linked Sonnet 70. (The poet's apparent vindication of his friend in Sonnet 70, which is generally overstressed because of careless reading, cannot be

35

overlooked, but it may be set aside for the present.)
Perhaps the strongest censure is conveyed by the
twelfth line, "To thy fair flower add the *rank smell
of weeds,*" if one may gauge the moral weight of its
imagery partly by the sestet of Sonnet 94, especially
the couplet:

> The summer's flow'r is to the summer sweet,
> Though to itself it only live and die;
> But if that flow'r with base infection meet,
> The basest weed outbraves his dignity:
>> For sweetest things turn sourest by their
>> deeds;
>> Lilies that fester smell far worse than
>> weeds.

A weed is not only common, useless, and perhaps harmful, but it also has a strong, foul, or even noxious odor.
The fact that its odor is "rank," a word signifying moral
disgust in a number of Shakespearean contexts,[17] is
what makes it particularly offensive. Line 13, "But why
thy odor matcheth not thy show," puts the opposition
of the preceding line in more general terms; for, on the
basis of Sonnets 5 (ll. 13–14) and 54, "odor" means
essence or essential part, the moral reality underlying
reputation, and not merely reputation as Tyler and
Tucker would have it, while "show" obviously denotes
mere physical appearance (as it does in Sonnets 5, 54,
and 93). Thus despite the whitewash applied in Sonnet
70, the imagery indicates that the basic disparity here
is not between beautiful appearance and ugly *reputation,* but rather between beautiful appearance and ugly
moral reality, as it is in another couplet (Sonnet 93)
ending with the same words:

> How like Eve's apple doth thy beauty *grow*
> If thy sweet *virtue* answer not thy *show!*

In the last line, "The soil is this, that thou dost common grow," the poet specifies the reason his friend's
odor does not match his show. "Soil," a widely accepted
emendation of the Quarto's "solye,"[18] is rich in meaning.

36

Continuing the imagery of the previous lines, it signifies earth or ground, the latter in turn suggesting ground in the sense of basis or foundation and hence reason; by way of the connection between earth and dirt, it also passes readily into the sense of (moral) blemish, spot, or stain. All these senses, which derive from the context and Shakespeare's linguistic habits, make the efforts of editors and lexicographers to assign "soil" the unique meaning of the solution to a problem quite superfluous.

Tucker's comments on "soil" and "common," indeed on the couplet as a whole, are so typical that they are worth quoting:

> The case is regarded as a problem which requires a 'soil' (= solution). The poet does not admit (see the next sonnet) that the beloved actually lacks the proper fragrance (cf. S. 5 and 54). The *real* 'solution' is that, though he possesses the odour, he makes it 'common' by being too free with his society; cf. 102.12 'Sweets grown common lose their dear delight.' 'Weeds' are the type of commonness, 'flowers' of choiceness. *Odour* = reputation. . . . For *Common* cf. Cor. 2.3.101. . . .[19]

Observe here the efforts of one who by his own admission gives full weight to Sonnet 70 to put the most favorable interpretation upon "weeds," "soil," and "common." The result is a gloss that really explains nothing, that leaves everything virtually as ambiguous as it was before. The last sentence is almost tautological: of course weeds are the type of commonness—the Sonnet makes that quite clear; but what *kind* of commonness? And how can the unfavorable implications of "rank smell of weeds" be ignored by one who has cited Sonnet 94 in connection with it? As for the friend's being too free with his society, there is more than one way to be too free: [20] one may balance the use of "common" in Sonnet 102 and *Coriolanus* by examples from Sonnet 137 (l. 10) and *Much Ado About Nothing* (IV.i.65).

The fact is, "common" has a fairly wide spectrum of

signification in Shakespeare's works, with pejorative meanings ranging from promiscuous in sexual relations (Sonnet 137) to "stale and cheap to vulgar company" (*I Henry IV*, III.ii.41). R. H. Case's query regarding "common" neatly sums up the reader's basic problem: "Is Shakespeare rebuking his friend for general loving, or merely . . . with gracing iniquity with his presence (see lxvii)?" [21] His reference to Sonnet 67 indicates that the issue does not hang upon "common," or even upon all of Sonnet 69, alone. Beginning with Sonnet 70, other contexts—for example, Sonnets 54, 67, 93–96, and 121—are brought to bear to support, or to help one arrive at, an interpretation. If one chooses to stress and take at its face value Sonnet 70, then like most of the commentators he will minimize the blame and take "common" as "stale and cheap to vulgar company" or gracing iniquity with his presence.[22] But if one reads Sonnet 70 warily and gives full weight to other relevant contexts, to the serious opposition of appearance and reality in Sonnets 54 and 93–96, to the imagery of these Sonnets and that of lines 12–14, as well as the moral implications of "rank" and "weed" in the plays, he will find strong disapproval in the poem and take "common" to mean promiscuous in sexual relations [23]—as I do.

Shakespeare's reluctance to blame a friend directly for sins committed may underlie the strategy of Sonnets 69 and 54 as well as Sonnets 93 and 94; his inclination to forgive a friend almost anything is evident in Sonnets 33–35 and 40–42.[24] This tendency to excuse a friend is also at work in Sonnet 70, which continues the sense of the preceding poem by representing its justified charge as slander:

> That thou art blamed shall not be thy defect,
> For slander's mark was ever yet the fair;
> The ornament of beauty is suspect,
> 4 A crow that flies in heaven's sweetest air.
> So thou be good, slander doth but approve
> Thy worth the greater, being wooed of time;

For canker vice the sweetest buds doth love,
8 And thou present'st a pure unstainèd prime.
Thou hast passed by the ambush of young
      days,
Either not assailed, or victor being charged;
Yet this thy praise cannot be so thy praise
12 To tie up envy, evermore enlarged.
   If some suspect of ill masked not thy show,
   Then thou alone kingdoms of hearts
      shouldst owe.[25]

The poet begins by assuring his friend that being cen-
sured for faults ought not to be taken as (necessarily)
the result of a personal blemish, for slander's target
always was and still is anyone who is beautiful (and un-
sullied). One might go so far as to say that suspicion is
the customary ornament of beauty: a black crow that
habitually flies in the purest air of heaven. The speaker
then proceeds to give some excellent advice. Provided
that the friend, who is tempted to immoral behavior by
the present times, be virtuous, slander will only prove
his merit to be the greater; for the worm of vice attacks
the sweetest young flowers, and the friend already
presents a spotless youth to the public eye. He has suc-
cessfully *passed by* the ambush of youth's proverbial
inclination to sins of the flesh,[26] and yet the praise he
rightly receives for this accomplishment cannot be so
lasting as to restrain permanently the Blatant Beast of
malice, which is always being set free. The poet ends as
he began—with a word of consolation. If some suspicion
of evil did not obscure his friend's beautiful appearance,
his case would be unique: then he alone would possess
the love and devotion of countless men.

The first quatrain of the Sonnet consists largely of
"transparent casuistry," to borrow Lever's phrase.[27]
"Shall" is used with the infinitive in the old sense of
"ought" [28]—a kind of moral imperative—while "defect"
parallels some of the meanings of "soil" in Sonnet 69.
The second line is a truism designed to provide a moral

basis for the first, but truisms are notoriously inapplicable in many particular cases. Here the ambiguity of "fair" allows the poet to pacify his friend and satisfy his own conscience at the same time,[29] for its senses range from the purely physical (beauty of appearance) to the purely moral (beauty of the unblemished mind). No one denies that the friend possesses physical beauty, but in view of Sonnet 69 one may doubt that unstained moral beauty now accompanies it. All beauty is subject to suspicion (l. 3), and yet it is an ornament only to moral beauty, a qualification which is made explicit in lines 5–6. It would not be unfair to regard "So" (if only, provided that) as emphatic and read it as "If and only if." "So thou be good" together with "being wooed of time" suggests the Protestant (and Senecan) ideal of tested virtue, which is realized in lines 9–10. In the case of "sweetest" (l. 7), unlike that of "fair," there is no need to distinguish between the categories of physical and moral attractiveness into which its senses fall, for its moral implications are sustained by lines 8–10. To put it differently, there is no reason to doubt that the poet's friend was both morally and physically fair and sweet in his "young days" or "prime."

To forestall objections, I must admit that "prime" and "young days" are certainly ambiguous references to age. "Prime" denotes that which is first either in time (the beginning) or in quality (the best), and it is associated with youth in at least five different contexts.[30] One of these passages is worth quoting because it includes the canker figure of Sonnet 70 and tends to support my equating "prime" with "young days":

> Yet writers say, as in the sweetest bud
> The eating canker dwells, so eating love
> Inhabits in the finest wits of all.
>
> And writers say, as the most forward bud
> Is eaten by the canker ere it blow,
> Even so by love the young and tender wit

Is turned to folly; blasting in the bud,
Losing his verdure even in the prime,
And all the fair effects of future hopes.[31]

The last six lines here could be regarded as a figurative description of what is happening to the person addressed in Sonnet 69. Most readers would perhaps argue that "young days" refers to an earlier stage of youth than "prime" on the strength of a few contexts [32] and the temporally ambiguous "present'st"; but there are equally good reasons for the view that "prime" and "young days" have the same temporal reference. For example, a common feature of Shakespeare's method is the expansion, explanation, or variation of something that has been said.[33] Without straining syntax or sense, one may regard lines 9–10 as an explanatory expansion of line 8, and the whole third quatrain as an explanatory expansion of the second. In any case, the tone and feeling of the whole Sonnet are against taking line 8 as a flat assertion of the friend's blamelessness *at this moment.*

Even a casual reading of Sonnet 70 should suggest that it is by no means the complete reversal of Sonnet 69 it is generally taken to be. Considered as a defense, it is quite lukewarm and cautious, a masterpiece of conscious or unconscious equivocation if only because Shakespeare loves the person though he hates the vice. There are stong indications in each of the quatrains of reservations and qualifications in the mind of the poet, and the strongest affirmation of his friend's innocence (ll. 8–10) applies not to the present but to his past. In the second quatrain the conditional phrase "So thou be good" is a reminder and warning to the friend that he must be virtuous *now* if he is to survive the test of slander. A similar reminder is introduced by "Yet" in the third quatrain, the point of lines 11–12 being not merely that praise can never hope to overcome malice, but also that praise for *past* virtue cannot counteract malice as the present and perennial cause of slander.[34]

41

III

Before I offer my interpretation of Sonnets 53 and 54, I
shall try to place them in a tentative group beginning
with Sonnet 43, "When most I wink, then do mine eyes
best see," and ending perhaps with Sonnet 58, "That
god forbid that made me first your slave." The common
factor which these Sonnets share is that they are all
written in absence, and their descriptive and emotive
meaning derives from the poet's separation from his
friend. As far as one can tell, it is the speaker who is
away from friend and home in most of these Sonnets,
but in Sonnets 56–58 the friend is absent in pursuit of
pleasure. There are five islands of linked Sonnets (44–
45, 46–47, 50–51, 53–55, 57–58) within this large, loose,
and moderately varied group. I shall survey it rapidly,
quoting only those poems which are significant for the
reading of Sonnets 53 and 54.

The opening Sonnet, 43, may speak for itself:

When most I wink, then do mine eyes best
    see,
For all the day they view things unrespected;
But when I sleep, in dreams they look on
    thee
4 And, darkly bright, are bright in dark
    directed.
Then thou, whose shadow shadows doth
    make bright,
How would thy shadow's form form happy
    show
To the clear day with thy much clearer light
8 When to unseeing eyes thy shade shines so!
How would, I say, mine eyes be blessèd
    made
By looking on thee in the living day,
When in dead night thy fair imperfect shade
12 Through heavy sleep on sightless eyes doth
    stay!

All days are nights to see till I see thee,
And nights bright days when dreams do
    show thee me.[35]

It is followed by a pair of poor Sonnets employing the four elements. In 44, "If the dull substance of my flesh were thought," the poet regrets that the heavy and inert elements of his body, earth and water, are not "nimble thought" so that he could instantly leap any distance and be with his friend. Sonnet 45, "The other two, slight air and purging fire," turns to the lighter elements, air and fire, which are equated with the poet's thought and desire, and whose recurrent absence more or less accounts for his being sad, "so much of earth and water wrought." Sonnets 46 and 47 concern the relationships between the speaker's eye and heart, the first presenting their quarrel and its resolution, the second their cooperative alliance. Sonnet 46, "Mine eye and heart are at a mortal war," describes a legal action between eye and heart over the sight of his friend, each arguing that it alone contains his image; a jury of thoughts decides that the friend's "outward part" is the eye's due, the heart's his fervent "inward love." [36] In Sonnet 47, "Betwixt mine eye and heart a league is took," the poet's eye and heart have made an alliance and now do good turns for each other in accordance with the verdict in Sonnet 46's couplet: the eye's province is the friend's portrait, the heart's function is to provide "thoughts of love." Fears that his friend, his dearest possession, may be stolen in his absence are expressed in Sonnet 48:

How careful was I, when I took my way,
Each trifle under truest bars to thrust,
That to my use it might unusèd stay
4   From hands of falsehood, in sure wards of
        trust!
But thou, to whom my jewels trifles are,
Most worthy comfort, now my greatest grief,
Thou, best of dearest and mine only care,

8   Art left the prey of every vulgar thief.
      Thee have I not locked up in any chest,
      Save where thou art not, though I feel thou
        art,
      Within the gentle closure of my breast,
12   From whence at pleasure thou mayst come
        and part;
      And even thence thou wilt be stol'n, I fear,
      For truth proves thievish for a prize so
        dear.

The next poem, "Against that time (if ever that time come)," is the first of the group to make no mention of absence, but its anticipation of the time when the poet's friend may choose to leave him seems to arise quite naturally from the anxiety of Sonnet 48. Shakespeare is slowly and reluctantly riding away from his friend in 50 and 51, Sonnets which have relatively little imagery. Sonnet 50, "How heavy do I journey on the way," emphasizing the speaker's grief, conveys the dispirited weariness of both horse and rider; Sonnet 51, "Thus can my love excuse the slow offense," contrasts the present excusable slowness of his horse with the speed he will require on the return journey, when nothing can keep pace with his desire. Making the best of their separation, in Sonnet 52 he suggests that even absence has its advantages, for the time which keeps his friend from him will make "some special instant special blest."

      So am I as the rich whose blessèd key
      Can bring him to his sweet up-lockèd
        treasure,
      The which he will not ev'ry hour survey,
4   For blunting the fine point of seldom
        pleasure.
      Therefore are feasts so solemn and so rare,
      Since, seldom coming, in the long year set,
      Like stones of worth they thinly placèd are,
8   Or captain jewels in the carcanet.
      So is the time that keeps you as my chest,

> Or as the wardrobe which the robe doth
> hide,
> To make some special instant special blest
> 12 By new unfolding his imprisoned pride.
> Blessèd are you, whose worthiness gives
> scope,
> Being had, to triumph, being lacked, to
> hope.

There are no references to separation or absence in Sonnets 53–55, and yet this comment on 53 is not unjustified, as I shall attempt to make clear: "Not being able, *in absence,* to possess his friend, he finds his friend's shadow in all beautiful things." [37] The implications of Sonnet 53's couplet are continued and expanded in Sonnet 54, which in turn is connected to the eternizing Sonnet 55. A new note is introduced by 56, a Sonnet in the optative "mood"; "Sweet love, renew thy force; be it not said / Thy edge should blunter be than appetite." [38] Apparently, the friend's sexual appetite has begun to displace his love for the poet, hence Shakespeare urges a renewal of the strength of the friend's affection. The "sad int'rim" separating them is not a mere absence but rather an estrangement. With the master-slave Sonnets 57 and 58 the worst fears of Sonnet 48 have been realized, and the enslaved poet is forced to endure full-blown inconstancy and deliberate desertion.[39]

In order to support the view that Sonnet 53 (and thus Sonnet 54) is "written in absence" and belongs to this group, it will be necessary to compare some Sonnets which partially resemble it and/or contain the word "shadow." The results of such a comparison are most conveniently summarized by a table (see p. 46).

A glance at these Sonnets should convince one that it is only when they are separated that Shakespeare dwells upon shadows or images of a friend—at best a poor substitute for the living presence, as Sonnets 43, 97, and 98 make clear. Absence causes the poet's loving imagi-

Sonnet	Shadow (and related words or ideas)	Absence
27	"my soul's imaginary sight / Presents thy *shadow*"	"my thoughts *from far where I abide*"
37	"this *shadow* doth such substance give"	By connection with Sonnet 36 ("separable spite") [40]
43	*shadow* (3X), *shade* (2X), *form*	"All days are nights to see *till I see thee*" (Sonnets 43–52, 56–58)
53	*shadow* (3X), *shade, counterfeit, substance*	
61	*shadows, image, spirit*	"So far from home," "From me far off"
98	"*figures* of delight, / Drawn after you, you *pattern* of all those. . . . As with your *shadow* I with these did play."	"From you I have been absent in the spring"
99	"More flowers I noted, yet I none could see / But sweet or color it had stol'n from thee."	By connection with Sonnet 98
113	"Mine eye" . . . "shapes" all things "to your feature."	*Since I left you*

nation, in coöperation with memory, to create an image of the friend and to find, or rather project, many images of the friend's beauty in his surroundings. Thus it is at least highly probable that the thought and feeling of Sonnet 53, like those of the other poems using "shadow," stem from absence.

Sonnet 53, because of its diction and provenience, might be called one of the most Platonic of the Sonnets. Universally regarded as a piece of unqualified praise, it exhibits the following structure: a Platonic generalization in the first quatrain is illustrated by particulars in the second and third; the twelfth line, which gives a rough summary of the sense, is restated by the thirteenth, while the last line presents a novel climax.

> What is your substance, whereof are you
>   made,
> That millions of strange shadows on you
>   tend?
> Since every one hath, every one, one shade,
> 4 And you, but one, can every shadow lend.
> Describe Adonis, and the counterfeit
> Is poorly imitated after you.
> On Helen's cheek all art of beauty set,
> 8 And you in Grecian tires are painted new.
> Speak of the spring and foison of the year:
> The one doth shadow of your beauty show,
> The other as your bounty doth appear,
> 12 And you in every blessèd shape we know.
> In all external grace you have some part,
> But you like none, none you, for constant
>   heart.

The opening quatrain, depending on the distinction between shadow and substance as well as various senses of shadow, has Shakespeare asking the handsome youth,[41] What is your essence, what makes you what you are, that millions of images not your own serve or wait on you? For everyone has only one shadow, and you, though but one, can give rise to every image (of

47

the millions which serve you). For example, describe Adonis, and the word picture of that perfect male turns out to be a poor imitation of you; enhance Helen's natural beauty as much as possible, and you are represented anew in Grecian attire (ll. 5–8).[42] Or speak of spring and of autumn, season of plenty; spring seems the image of your beauty, fall of your generosity. Indeed, we recognize you in every form blessed with beauty (ll. 9–12). You have some share in all external beauty (for you are in a sense its Idea), but you are like no one, and no one is like you, in regard to constancy of heart.

"Substance" signifies essence or the nature of a thing, *"quod stat subtus,* that which stands beneath, and (as it were) supports, the appearance";[43] also, in accordance with the expansion in the last half of the line, it denotes the material of which something is made. "Shadow" plays on several senses: body's silhouette (the "shade" of l. 3); image, reflection, likeness; and picture or portrait (the "counterfeit" of l. 5). In Plato's *Symposium* (212a) the difference between the Idea of Beauty, which is sole and absolute, and all other beauties is put in terms of the disparity between substance and shadow,[44] truth and mere images or reflections of it; and "shadow" is virtually a technical term of the Neoplatonism of Shakespeare's time:

> 'Shadow' and 'reflexion' were used by renaissance Platonists as alternative metaphors in expounding Plato's doctrine that Beauty which we see is the copy of an eternal pattern—Giordano Bruno had discoursed in Paris *De Umbris Idearum. . . .*[45]

In short, the poem's principal conceit, that all *external* beauty consists of mere shadows of the youth's "perfect" Beauty, may derive from metaphysical Platonism. This conceit is ostensibly enriched by the attribution of bounty and transcended or made even more Platonic in the last line by the attribution of unique constancy.[46]

Although in one sense the liberality of the handsome

youth is explained by the fourth line—he lends all the images of his beauty that the poet sees—the sphere in which his bounty operates is not otherwise defined. But with "foison" as its "image," his generosity inevitably recalls Antony, who was generous as lover, friend, and ruler: "For his bounty, / There was no winter in't, an autumn 'twas / That grew the more by reaping" (*Antony and Cleopatra*, V.ii.86–88). These lines in turn remind us of Juliet, whose bounty was also infinite, though restricted to the sphere of love: "My bounty is as boundless as the sea, / My love as deep; the more I give to thee, / The more I have, for both are infinite" (*Romeo and Juliet*, II.ii.133–135). One assumes, then, that the youth is generous in the personal relations of friendship and love, which is highly commendable and desirable as long as he is constant; but as the sexual implications of "liberal," "frank," and "free" may suggest,[47] giving freely and generously of oneself is also a necessary condition of inconstancy.

The fact that bounty may not be a pure blessing is hardly enough to justify the qualms one is likely to feel about taking the last line at its face value. Nor is it enough to be "struck by the inapplicability of this tribute to the personage addressed in 35, 40–42, and others."[48] Still, one is inclined to suspect that there is unconscious irony in the assertion and to ask, Why talk about constancy; isn't it usually taken for granted—when it actually exists? The answer is not to be found in J. B. Leishman's suggestion of a conventional borrowing from Ronsard:

> Despite the 'conventional' allusions to Adonis and Helen in Shakespeare's sonnet, I must confess that I have always been rather surprised by the conventional triteness of the concluding couplet. . . . Why just here should Shakespeare 'drag in' (as one might be inclined to say) the all too familiar 'constant heart'? Perhaps because he had this sonnet of Ronsard's in mind:
>
> Icy un coeur constant, qu'on ne peut esbranler.[49]

Contexts within the absence group furnish answers to this question and some justification of one's doubts, for when the poet's hyperbolic statement is examined in the light of Sonnets 48, 49, 52, 54, and 56–58, one must conclude that it probably springs less from an attitude of confident assurance than from one of fearful hope.

The sense of its couplet clearly links Sonnet 53 to the next poem: assertion of the youth's extraordinary beauty and "constancy" leads to Sonnet 54's homily on the relative importance of external beauty and beauty which has the moral center of truth—troth, constancy, loyalty, fidelity. This poem also approximates the structure of Sonnet 53, since the initial generalization is illustrated by the particular contrasting examples of the sweet rose and the odorless dog-rose (ll. 3–12), with application of the rose to the case of the beauteous and lovely youth being made in the couplet.

> O, how much more doth beauty beauteous
> seem
> By that sweet ornament which truth doth
> give!
> The rose looks fair, but fairer we it deem
> 4 For that sweet odor which doth in it live.
> The canker blooms have full as deep a dye
> As the perfumèd tincture of the roses,
> Hang on such thorns, and play as wantonly
> 8 When summer's breath their maskèd buds
> discloses;
> But, for their virtue only is their show,
> They live unwooed and unrespected fade,
> Die to themselves. Sweet roses do not so:
> 12 Of their sweet deaths are sweetest odors
> made.
> And so of you, beauteous and lovely
> youth,
> When that shall vade, by verse distills
> your truth.

Beginning his homily with an exclamation of how much external beauty is enhanced and completed by constancy, Shakespeare chooses the rose as the emblem of such beauty. This traditionally loveliest of flowers has both a fair appearance and a sweet odor that is internal and integral (ll. 1–4). As the emblem of mere external beauty he takes the odorless wild dog rose, which has all the other qualities of the rose (ll. 5–8). But because the excellence and essence of these canker blooms lies in their appearance alone, they are utterly neglected, living and dying for and by themselves and leaving nothing behind. Sweet roses, on the other hand, do not live and die in neglect: from their sweet corpses the sweetest odors are distilled (ll. 9–12). And in the same way, when the beauty of the lovable and loving youth shall perish, his essential beauty (truth) shall be preserved by poetry.

Throughout the Sonnet "sweet" has its full range of meaning, though its identification with truth puts the emphasis on its moral senses. The sweet ornament which truth or constancy gives is not an ornament of the ordinary kind usually associated with appearance or show and condemned in *The Merchant of Venice* (III.ii.74–100); instead, it is like the sweet odor of the rose which "doth *in* it *live*." In the second quatrain "dye" and "tincture" both denote color or hue, and "maskèd," a metaphor from social custom, seems devoid of moral implications. However, "hang on" and "*play* as *wantonly*" in line 7 may have sexual connotations suggesting the kind of sexual freedom that is undesirable because incompatible with constancy.[50] Since "virtue" in the third quatrain has the senses good quality or property and substance, essence, essential part, it is partially equivalent to "substance" in Sonnet 53; and line 9 as a whole is one of several reminders of the moral contrast between appearance and reality, odor (or virtue) and show [51] which runs through the poem.

The genuine and not unwarranted fears that underlie

this homiletic Sonnet seem close to the surface in lines 10–11. Although line 12 may suggest that the last half of line 11, "Sweet roses do not so," refers primarily to its first half, "Die to themselves," both syntax and sense allow us to include line 10 within the scope of its reference. Thus, though canker blooms "live unwooed and unrespected fade," sweet roses do not; they are frequently wooed and all too much respected or regarded, and therein lies the reason for the poet's fears and hopes regarding constancy. He has already made it clear in Sonnet 48 that he fears that in his absence the rose, the beauteous youth, may be not only wooed but stolen: "Thou . . . / Art left the prey of every vulgar thief"; "thou wilt be stol'n, I fear, / For truth proves thievish for a prize so dear." And how difficult, or rather impossible, it is to resist the temptation of being wooed is conveyed by the octave of Sonnet 41:

> Those pretty wrongs that liberty commits
> When I am sometime absent from thy
> > heart,
> Thy beauty and thy years full well befits,
> For still temptation follows where thou art.
> Gentle thou art, and therefore to be won;
> Beauteous thou art, therefore to be assailed;
> And when a woman woos, what woman's son
> Will sourly leave her till she have prevailed?

But what can the absent poet do to preserve the youth's truth, the most cherished value of the Sonnets? [52] He can only write this poem in which he is "hoping the best and giving precept in the form of praise," to quote Beeching's comment on Sonnet 70, concluding with the offer of a future reward. He will reward the youth by eternizing him through poetry, whose power to preserve him till Judgment Day is expatiated on in Sonnet 55, "Not marble nor the gilded monuments." This offer is not a bribe, if only because virtue as truth is its own reward: only if he is sweet or true can *anything* attractive be preserved, for his beauty or show must inevitably perish.

I think one may now perceive that Sonnets 53–55, which at first seem to constitute a sharp digression in an absence group, spring quite as much from separation as do the other poems, and in fact mark a stage in a psychological progression beginning with Sonnet 48. Here venting of the fear that his friend will be stolen is actually a euphemistic way of saying, I'm afraid you will prove inconstant. It is only a slight step from this transparent doubt to anticipation of complete loss in Sonnet 49, with its mixture of self-assertion and self-abnegation. In Sonnet 52 the fear of satiety which is all too apparent may be referred to the poet himself, but it is more likely to be the result of the friend's attitude and another way of doubting his fidelity. Sonnets 53 and 54 finally bring the matter into the open by optimistically attributing constancy to the handsome youth; yet, despite the confidence ostensibly imparted by the sense of these poems, the speaker's doubts and fears probably outweigh his hopes. Sonnet 53 stresses the youth's exceptional beauty, the one thing that Shakespeare (like the tongues of Sonnet 69) can be sure of. Its climax ascribes an even more exceptional constancy to him for obvious reasons: to be unusually handsome is to be unusually tempted; *ergo* to be true under such conditions must require a loyalty virtually unique. A homily [53] on constancy as *essential* beauty follows; needless to say, no one delivers a sermon to a person who doesn't need it. In short, the initial query of Sonnet 53—What is your *substance?*— is no more answered by Sonnet 54 than by its own last line, for the doubts and fears remain, to be borne out by the Sonnets after 55. The satiety feared in 52 enters with Sonnet 56 as lust overcomes love, and with Sonnets 57 and 58 the drama ends in flagrant inconstancy and cruel desertion.

Perhaps it is easier to accept my view of Sonnets 53

and 54, 69 and 70 if one remembers that the *general* technique used in these pairs is not new but rather old and familiar. Beeching summed it up briefly when he said that the speaker is "hoping the best and giving precept in the form of praise." The writers of the Renaissance, trained in rhetoric from grammar school on, would consider these poems typical specimens of epideictic rhetoric, the literature of praise and blame. In one of several interesting passages on this kind of rhetoric, Aristotle offers what might be taken as a *general* description of what Shakespeare seems to be doing in these Sonnets—suggesting by praising:

> Praise and counsels have a common aspect; for what you might suggest in counselling becomes encomium by a change in the phrase. Accordingly, when we know what we ought to do and the qualities we ought to possess, we ought to make a change in the phrase and turn it, employing this knowledge as a suggestion. For instance, the statement that "one ought not to pride oneself on goods which are due to fortune, but on those which are due to oneself alone," when expressed in this way, has the force of a suggestion; but expressed thus, "he was proud, not of goods which were due to fortune, but of those which were due to himself alone," it becomes praise. Accordingly, if you desire to praise, look what you would suggest; if you desire to suggest, look what you would praise.[54]

A comment in Bacon's essay "Of Praise" puts it more briefly and bluntly: "some praises come of good wishes and respects, which is a form due in civility to kings and great persons, *laudando praecipere*, when by telling men what they are, they represent to them what they should be." [55] And C. S. Lewis notes that an established feature of Renaissance encomiastic verse was that it "hid advice as flattery and recommended virtues by feigning that they already existed." [56]

Shakespeare would agree with the epigraphs to this

54

chapter and with Spenser's assertion that the "trew fayre . . . is the gentle wit and vertuous mind" (*Amoretti*, No. 79),[57] but he also recognizes that "nature with a beauteous wall / Doth oft close in pollution" (*Twelfth Night*, I.ii.46–47). Characteristically he asks in Sonnet 92, "what's so blessèd-fair that fears no blot," and he is inclined to feel that inconstancy is often a concomitant of physical beauty.[58] Among the Sonnets which deal with this disparity between physical appearance and moral reality are Sonnets 93–96, 69 and 70, 53 and 54. It is no accident that in most of them we are confronted by ambiguities of one sort or another, for there are evidently diverse attitudes and emotions simultaneously at work in the poet's mind. His self-respect, firm beliefs, love of a friend, disposition to forgive offenses and faults, and other factors in his mind and personal relationships set up tensions which are occasionally fairly obvious, though more often below the surface, and which result in ambiguity of meaning. There are other Sonnets whose tensions are more evident and just as interesting, and I shall next discuss some of these poems, in which strong conflicting feelings produce a veritable civil war in the poet.

3

The Civil War:
SONNETS 33–35, 40–42, AND 57–58

Such civil war is in my love and hate
That I an accessáry needs must be
To that sweet thief which sourly robs from me.
Sonnet 35

But, for those earthly faults, I quit them all,
And pray thee take this mercy to provide
For better times to come.
Measure for Measure

That vigilant, besetting, insatiable affection, so full of doubts and torments, with which the lover follows his object, is out of place here; for the friend has no property in his friend's body or leisure or residual ties; he accepts what is offered and what is acceptable, and the rest he leaves in peace. He is distinctly not his brother's keeper, for the society of friends is free.
George Santayana, *Reason in Society*

They provide a very good exemplification of that ambivalence in feeling which governs most of our intimate relationships with other human beings.
Sigmund Freud

THE SPEAKER's mixed feelings about his friend, his simultaneous liking and disliking, his being attracted and repelled, are apparent in the octave of Sonnet 94. The negative component of this ambivalence is perceptibly stronger than the positive one, and indeed it seems

56

reasonable to suppose that in most instances of ambivalence one state of mind will outweigh the other. At any
rate, such is generally the case in the three sets of Sonnets which I shall now consider, for, although both affection and antagonism may be quite evident, the poet at
different times seems to give more emphasis to either his
positive or negative feelings.

Sonnets 33–35 comprise a small group in which the
poet makes it clear that he has been offended by the
masculine friend he addresses and that he is willing to
forgive him. These basic facts, a sense of injury and a
disposition to forgive, fix the poles between which the
speaker's feelings move. Each of the Sonnets ends with
some assurance of forgiveness, but in the first it is given
rather freely, in the second with more difficulty, and in
the last very reluctantly. In short, as this progression
may suggest, there is an increase in the intensity and
complexity of the speaker's feelings as we pass from one
poem to another. Sonnet 33, "Full many a glorious morn-
ing have I seen," the simplest in tone and feeling, mini-
mizes the poet's distress, partly by its felicities of description; Sonnet 34, "Why didst thou promise such a
beauteous day," reproaches the friend in unanswerable
terms, and yet concludes with a sudden reversal; Sonnet 35, "No more be grieved at that which thou hast
done," sets forth the conflict within the poet, revealing
the strength of the opposed impulses.

To use the language of Sonnet 35 (l. 6), Shakespeare
is simply authorizing his friend's trespass by comparisons in Sonnet 33, a poem which is organized as an extended simile containing metaphors within each of its
members:

> Full many a glorious morning have I seen
> Flatter the mountain tops with sovereign
> eye,
> Kissing with golden face the meadows
> green,

4   Gilding pale streams with heavenly alchemy;
Anon permit the baset clouds to ride
With ugly rack on his celestial face,
And from the fórlorn world his visage hide,
8   Stealing unseen to west with this disgrace.
Even so my sun one early morn did shine
With all-triumphant splendor on my brow;
But, out alack! he was but one hour mine,
12   The region cloud hath masked him from me
      now.
    Yet him for this my love no whit
      disdaineth;
    Suns of the world may stain when
      heaven's sun staineth.

Two Renaissance commonplaces, the sun-king comparison and the sun-son word play, are put to such good use in the friend's behalf that "out alack," the emphatic [1] but conventional phrase denoting the speaker's regret, seems no more than a polite formula. The excuse offered in the couplet [2] may be unconvincing in view of the next two Sonnets, but it is so plausible within the limits of this one that the quatrains seem to exist mainly to provide grounds for it. Yet there are also signs of disapproval: "basest," "ugly," and "disgrace" are strong pejoratives which may have been elicited by the friend's fault,[3] and when applied to "suns of the world," "stain" signifies become soiled or blemished [4] as well as grow dim, become obscured.

Sonnet 34 continues the sense of the previous poem—for its first six lines by means of metaphors with the same or similar vehicles: [5]

    Why didst thou promise such a beauteous
      day
    And make me travel forth without my cloak,
    To let base clouds o'ertake me in my way,
4   Hiding thy brav'ry in their rotten smoke?
    'Tis not enough that through the cloud thou
      break

To dry the rain on my storm-beaten face,
For no man well of such a salve can speak
8 That heals the wound, and cures not the
       disgrace:
Nor can thy shame give physic to my grief;
Though thou repent, yet I have still the loss.
Th' offender's sorrow lends but weak relief
12 To him that bears the strong offense's cross.
   Ah, but those tears are pearl which thy
       love sheeds,
   And they are rich and ransom all ill
       deeds.[6]

After the first quatrain's rhetorical question,[7] calculated
to bring home to the friend his perfidy, the speaker reveals the depth of his grief and humiliation, especially
by the change to the comparisons of lines 7–9.[8] Throughout the second and third quatrains he reminds the offender of the inadequacy of consolation and repentance
after the fact; still, he feels that, because they are shed
out of love, his friend's tears are "pearl"[9] valuable
enough to "ransom all ill deeds." This apparent reversal
of tone and feeling is suspiciously abrupt, and one may
doubt that an access of loving forgiveness has actually
overcome the justifiably strong resentment displayed
in the quatrains.

   One of the most interesting and most discussed of the
poems appearing early in the collection, Sonnet 35 is a
continuation of 34 in the sense that it takes as its point
of departure the friend's sorrow, which the poet now
ostensibly attempts to allay.

   No more be grieved at that which thou hast
       done:
   Roses have thorns, and silver fountains mud;
   Clouds and eclipses stain both moon and
       sun,
4 And loathsome canker lives in sweetest bud.
   All men make faults, and even I in this,
   Authórizing thy trespass with compare,

59

Myself corrupting, salving thy amiss,
8 Excusing thy sins more than thy sins are;
For to thy sensual fault I bring in sense—
Thy adverse party is thy advocate—
And 'gainst myself a lawful plea commence.
12 Such civil war is in my love and hate
That I an accessáry needs must be
To that sweet thief which sourly robs
from me.

In the first quatrain his efforts to assuage his friend's grief consist of a series of emblematic and proverbial commonplaces which take one temporarily in the direction of Sonnet 33, as the example of the third line and the comment of the sixth indicate. The point of this series is that "no perfection is so absolute, / That some impurity doth not pollute," [10] but the third and fourth lines suggest the (moral) disapproval—note "stain" and "loathsome"—which breaks into the open in the second quatrain. Though line 5 appears to continue the general excuses, there is a marked shift in rhythm as the speaker becomes self-conscious,

All men make faults, and even I in this,

and from here on he fully objectifies the conflict within him. All men commit offenses, even the speaker in justifying his friend's trespass by the comparisons of lines 2–4 (and those of Sonnet 33 and the couplet of 34), corrupting himself while palliating his friend's misdeed (ll. 5–7).[11] For to extenuate the sensual fault he brings in not merely common sense but reason or judgment; thus the plaintiff, the injured party, through reason, the traditional opponent of passion, becomes the friend's counsel and begins a lawful plea against himself (ll. 9–11). The conflict between his love for the friend and hatred of his fault is such that he is compelled to be an accessary after the fact to the attractive offender (ll. 12–14).

The eighth line constitutes a special problem which must be treated in some detail. In the Quarto this line runs "Excusing their sins more than their sins are," and hence it is clearly incompatible with the rest of the poem. Mr. Rollins, like most modern editors, follows Capell and Malone in emending it to "Excusing thy sins more than thy sins are," a reading which is acceptable on the general grounds that a frequent mistake in the 1609 text of the Sonnets is the use of "their" for "thy." [12] However, to judge from the comments of some of its interpreters, this version is hardly more intelligible than the Quarto's. For example, although praised by Alden and adopted by a number of other editors, Steevens' vague gloss, "Making the excuse more than proportioned to the offence," [13] if I understand it correctly, invests the line with a meaning that is the reverse of what the Sonnet as a whole demands. The excuse is not greater than the fault, nor are the excuses simply more numerous than the faults; [14] the speaker is quite aware that the sins are too serious to be excused or whitewashed by the trivial commonplaces which he enumerates. Verity recognizes this in his sensible comment, "Making thy sins more excusable than they really are," [15] which apparently regards the line as elliptical—Excusing thy sins more than thy sins are (excusable)—and gives some necessary critical support to the prevalent text.

A more conservative emendation of the line, "Excusing thy sins, more than their sins are," first proposed by Wyndham and recently supported by C. J. Sisson, yields an interpretation that is somewhat similar to Verity's. Wyndham believes that "than their sins are" refers back to "All men make faults" and presumably takes "more" to mean greater; [16] hence he paraphrases the sense of the quatrain as follows:

> All men make faults, and even I in saying so, giving authority for thy trespass by thus comparing it to

> the faults of all men; I myself am guilty of cor-
> rupting in so "salving thy amiss"; excusing thy sins
> (which are) more than their sins are.[17]

Since "compare" refers to what is going on in lines 2–5, it is possible to take "their" (l. 8) as referring to the objects in lines 2–4 as well as to "all men," but Wyndham (unlike Sisson) avoids the temptation. However, he overlooks the fact that "myself corrupting," which may be read in two different ways, is more likely to signify corrupting myself than myself corrupting (you) in view of both meter and context. Like a doctor who contracts his patient's contagious disease, the poet is corrupting himself, lowering his own moral standards, by salving the friend's fault, by excusing sins which are greater than the venial ones all men commit.

Beeching rejects Steevens' explanation with the remark that "the poet blames the offence, only he blames the excuse even more," and his plausible interpretation of this line stresses its relation to the next:

> The necessary sense is plain from the line which
> follows. The poet sins worse than his friend be-
> cause in his excuse he sins against reason; and this
> can be got out of the reading "Excusing thy sins
> more than thy sins are," by taking "more" in the
> sense of "worse." . . .[18]

The poet sins against reason when, overturning the traditional hierarchy, he makes his intellect subservient to his own passions or emotions as well as to those of the friend as represented by his sensual fault. Of course the poet is as bad as, or worse than, the friend only according to ethical theory, but the hyperbole that Beeching's gloss entails is quite consonant with his disgust with himself for authorizing, salving, and excusing his friend's sins, and it makes the series in the second quatrain a crescendo of self-accusation.

"Trespass," "amiss," "sins," and "fault" are all strong pejoratives whose range of meaning allows them to be used interchangeably.[19] Its opposition to "sensual fault" controls the meaning of "sense" and points up the play on sensuality, and yet the larger context indicates that, in addition to denoting reason, judgment, understanding, common sense, it signifies a kind of understanding based on feeling. There is a certain irony in "lawful plea," for law should be on his side rather than the friend's, and the phrase not only suggests that sense works in lawful, orderly fashion but also that the excuses given in lines 2–5 exemplify a general law. "Sweet," clearly devoid of any favorable moral implications, and "sourly" provide a final reminder of the conflict in the poet by a characteristic easy antithesis.

From line 5 on Shakespeare has been hammering on essentially the same point in different ways, by means of different comparisons. Caught in the trap of his sympathetic understanding, he is compelled both to excuse his friend and to blame himself for doing so. What the friend has done to offend him we do not know; we only know that he has committed a sensual fault, although the imagery of line 14 *may* imply an offense similar to, or the same as, that of Sonnets 40–42.[20] In any case, the poet is venting negative feelings which are turned against himself chiefly because he is unable to direct them toward his friend. He is thus an unwilling accessary to the sin, and if he cannot rebuke his friend he can at least proclaim his own guilt.[21]

II

Sonnets 40–42, a trio of poems in which the speaker comments on aspects of a sexual triangle, have given biographical, psychological, and moral speculators as well as the perennial rearrangers almost unlimited opportunity for exercising their talents. The greatest temptation faced by editors and commentators is to link these three Sonnets with three others in which the speaker also comments on the relationships of persons caught in a sexual triangle, the paired Sonnets 133 and 134, "Beshrew that heart that makes my heart to groan"

63

and "So, now I have confessed that he is thine," and Sonnet 144, "Two loves I have, of comfort and despair." [22] The customary way of connecting all three sets of poems is to assume that the same friend and the same mistress are participants in each of the "dramas," and it is equally common to note that Sonnets 40–42 belong to the Dark Lady group (127–154) and then to rearrange them accordingly. No one would wish to deny that all six poems have sexual intrigue as their lowest common denominator and that the participants may be the same; still, one should also be aware of certain elementary differences between them. For example, in Sonnets 40–42 the poet addresses a handsome youth who has betrayed him by having sexual relations with his mistress; in Sonnets 133–134 he addresses a woman who has sexually enslaved his friend and him; in Sonnet 144 he addresses the world at large on the character and relations of his fair friend and his dark mistress. Furthermore, there are evident differences in tone and texture; except for a few lines in the first poem, Sonnets 40–42 have relatively little imagery, while there are many comparisons in the three later poems. In short, once one has paid his respects to the obvious possibilities of relationship, there is no compelling reason for discussing all these Sonnets together.

Throughout Sonnet 40 the poet manifests the ambivalence of his attitude toward the friend who stole his mistress. Forgiveness prevails, yet he can neither forgive nor blame wholeheartedly:

> Take all my loves, my love, yea, take them all!
> What hast thou then more than thou hadst before?
> No love, my love, that thou mayst true love call;
> 4 All mine was thine before thou hadst this more.
> Then, if for my love thou my love receivest,

I cannot blame thee for my love thou usest;
But yet be blamed if thou thyself deceivest.
8 By wilful taste of what thyself refusest.
I do forgive thy robb'ry, gentle thief,
Although thou steal thee all my poverty;
And yet love knows it is a greater grief
12 To bear love's wrong than hate's known in-
  jury.
  Lascivious grace, in whom all ill well
  shows,
  Kill me with spites; yet we must not be
  foes.[23]

The intensity of the speaker's bitter feeling in the first quatrain is conveyed by the emphasis of repetition, the monosyllables dinning into the friend's mind the fact that he has gained nothing more, nothing of value. Scornfully he invites his dear friend to take all his loves, his mistress as well as his affection, for all the good it will do him. He gets no more than he had before, no woman or relationship that he may call faithful or constant,[24] and all the poet's affection—or, everything of the poet's—was the friend's before this casual liaison.

With the second quatrain the technique of the last ten lines emerges: an assertion is made, then (sharply) modified by another assertion or clause introduced by an adversative ("But yet," "Although," "And yet," "yet"). Thus the grammatical structure as well as the sense of the Sonnet reveals the poet's mixed feelings. The second quatrain is notoriously difficult, partly because of the ambiguity of "for" and "my love" and the alternative readings "this self" and "thy self" in line 7. I shall offer two general interpretations of these lines, presenting first the one which I prefer: Since all my affection was yours,[25] if, in place of my love for you, you accept my mistress, I cannot blame you because you have sexual intercourse with her; yet you must be blamed if you cheat and delude me ("this selfe" of the Quarto) by a deliberate and lustful sampling of a

65

woman whom you do not love, whom you refuse to accept on any but a temporary basis. On this view the poet is saying to the friend that no one could blame him if he made a genuine choice between keeping the poet's love and sacrificing it for love of the poet's mistress; but, since he refused to commit himself to either course, he is seriously at fault—if only because he has cheated a friend.

This interpretation of the second quatrain recognizes that in terms of the first the "all mine" that "was thine" refers mainly to the speaker's unstinting love, or at least must exclude the mistress if "before" is taken seriously. However, most readers apparently regard "All mine was thine" as a variation of the old proverb, "Friends have all things in common," [26] or as a corollary to one of the basic commonplaces of the literature of friendship, "my friend and I are one" (Sonnet 42),[27] although the tone and feeling of the first quatrain are quite against this natural but routine response. For this majority the sense of the second quatrain must be approximately this: Since all that is mine is yours, if on account of my affection (for both of you) you admit my mistress into a familiar relationship with you (cf. 42, ll. 6–8), I can't blame you because you have sexual relations with her; [28] yet you must be blamed if you cheat and delude yourself by a deliberate and lustful enjoyment of a woman you do not love, whom you refuse to have as a wife.[29] To accept such an interpretation is to attribute to the speaker a capacity for self-sacrifice which is, to say the least, incredible.

In the third quatrain the poet tells the gentle thief that he is forgiven, even though he steals all of the little that he owns; [30] then he characteristically offsets his rather generous pardon by another reproof. Any lover recognizes that it is a greater hardship and injustice to endure a wrong inflicted by one who loves you than an injury resulting from overt hatred.[31] The mixed feelings implied by "gentle thief" are quite apparent in line

66

13, especially in the Ovidian phrase "Lascivious grace,"[32] but the understatement of the final clause indicates that friendship is stronger than sexual love.

"My love" signifies my dear friend, my mistress, my affection, while "love" as a relationship refers to the poet's devotion to his friend, his attachment to his mistress, and the friend's intercourse with her. "Take" is clearly related to "receivest," "usest," "taste," and "rob-b'ry" and may be said to comprehend them; in the same way "grief" (hardship, affliction, suffering—or the cause of them; grievance) includes the senses of "injury" and "wrong" and perhaps of "spites" also. "For" denotes on account of, in behalf of; in place or instead of; because; and "knows" signifies knows by direct experience as well as realizes, recognizes.

Dowden attempts to connect the less tortured and ambiguous Sonnet 41 with 40 by asserting, "The thought of XL.13, 'Lascivious grace, in whom all ill well shows,' is carried out in this sonnet"; Pooler merely notes that it continues the preceding poem.[33] There is something to be said for Dowden's statement, for "pretty wrongs" does recall "lascivious grace" in its balancing of censure and affection and it does pick up one of the key words of Sonnet 40; but the poems are so different that it is difficult to state the precise mode of continuation. At any rate, in the first eight lines of Sonnet 41 one finds the speaker temporarily turning from his unresolved feelings of resentment and forgiveness to a sympathetic and lucid attempt to account for his handsome young friend's libertinism.

> Those pretty wrongs that liberty commits
> When I am sometime absent from thy heart,
> Thy beauty and thy years full well befits,
> 4 For still temptation follows where thou art.
> Gentle thou art, and therefore to be won;
> Beauteous thou art, therefore to be assailed;
> And when a woman woos, what woman's son
> 8 Will sourly leave her till she have prevailed?

Ay me! but yet thou mightst my seat forbear,
And chide thy beauty and thy straying youth,
Who lead thee in their riot even there
12 Where thou art forced to break a twofold
truth:
Hers, by thy beauty tempting her to thee,
Thine, by thy beauty being false to me.[34]

It is possible to take the first two quatrains in a very general sense, regarding them as an indulgent analysis of the reasons for the youth's behavior on those occasions when he satisfies needs which friendship cannot fulfill, and having no necessary reference to his affair with the speaker's mistress. According to this view these eight lines serve simply as an essential introduction to the matter of real concern, which is dealt with in the third quatrain and the couplet, and hence the poet is able to call the friend's (other) sexual liaisons "pretty wrongs" (petty and attractive venial sins) and treat them as mere youthful indiscretions. He is saying, in effect, these amours are natural and understandable, but there is one woman you could and *should* have avoided.

The opposite interpretation, toward which many commentators are inclined, takes the first two quatrains as highly particular, referring primarily to wrongs the friend committed with the mistress during the poet's absence [35] and blaming them on his youth and beauty and her wooing. As Professor Hubler puts it after quoting lines 4–8, "the willing seduction of the youth is looked upon as the inevitable consequence of her attractive wantonness and of his youth and beauty." [36] It follows that readers of this school believe the poet refuses to hold his friend fully responsible for what has happened: "The young and handsome friend, tempted, is less culpable than the temptress. . . ." [37] They forget that this is a case in which one may profitably ask, like Angelo in *Measure for Measure*, "The tempter or the tempted, who sins most?"

68

Whatever view of the octave one may prefer, I think it is clear that in the last six lines of the Sonnet the poet counterbalances his previous lenient and fatherly attitude by a calm, regretful condemnation of the youth's betrayal of him and his mistress. Even here it will doubtless seem to many readers that the poet is inclined to divide the responsibility between the friend's free will (ll. 9–10) and his beauty and youth (ll. 11–14). Tucker goes so far as to say, "The poet lays the blame on the friend's beauty, not on his will. It is that beauty which tempts *her*, and is itself false to the poet," [38] probably because he favors the particular reading of the octave and stresses the verbs "lead" and "forced" here. But one must not forget that the sestet is a grammatical unit, with the main verbs in lines 9 and 10.[39] The emphasis is on the youth's personal responsibility for his actions, and the conjunction "but yet" must be given full weight. Alas, he reminds his friend, even though you are a handsome young libertine, you could (but do not) refrain from occupying *my* customary and rightful place; you could rebuke and restrain the beauty and youth which in their reckless pursuit of pleasure [40] lead you to my mistress, where you are "forced" to violate, by means of your beauty, a twofold allegiance to me: the constancy of her love and the constancy of your friendship.

Sonnet 42, the last and poorest of this group, is in some sense a continuation of 41, though it is hard to define their relationship. Perhaps one may say that referring to the unfaithfulness of friend and mistress at the end of one Sonnet leads the poet to compare their relative importance to him at the beginning of the next. He loved his mistress dearly and laments her loss, but the chief cause of his grief is the loss of his dear friend.

> That thou hast her, it is not all my grief,
> And yet it may be said I loved her dearly;
> That she hath thee is of my wailing chief,
> 4 A loss in love that touches me more nearly.
> Loving offenders, thus I will excuse ye:

Thou dost love her because thou know'st I
love her,
And for my sake even so doth she abuse me,
8 Suff'ring my friend for my sake to approve
her.
If I lose thee, my loss is my love's gain,
And losing her, my friend hath found that
loss:
Both find each other, and I lose both twain,
12 And both for my sake lay on me this cross.
But here's the joy—my friend and I are
one.
Sweet flattery! then she loves but me
alone.

In the second quatrain he proceeds to offer on behalf of
the "loving offenders" [41] an excuse recalling lines 5–6 of
Sonnet 40: they love each other for the poet's sake, his
mistress deceiving and injuring him by allowing his
friend to experience her sexual love ("approve her").[42]
He continues the excuse into the third quatrain in terms
of loss and gain, concluding it in the couplet with a
piece of bitter and desperate flattery or self-deception.

L. C. Knights, a perceptive reader of the Sonnets,
attributes the mediocrity of this one to Shakespeare's
profound lack of interest in what he is talking about:

The banal movement, the loose texture of the
verse, the vague gestures that stand for emotion,
are sufficient index that his interests are not very
deeply involved. (Contrast the run and ring of
the verse, even in minor sonnets, when Shakespeare is absorbed by his subject—"Devouring
time blunt thou the Lyons pawes . . .") His sole
interest is in the display of wit, the working out of
the syllogism.[43]

He then quotes lines 5–8 and 13–14 in support of his
point. I agree that the verse is banal, and the long excuse
is obviously feeble. I applaud Knights's efforts to dispose
of the biographical school of Sonnet criticism, but in

view of Sonnets 40 and 41 [44] I cannot agree that the poet's interests are not very deeply involved. On the contrary, it is because they are involved, because his feelings are running counter to his statements, that what he is saying (perhaps from line 5 on) carries no conviction. I hope it does not classify me as a naïve literalist of the biographical school to say that here the speaker is trying—and clearly without success—to accept disaster with good grace, probably because his attachment to his friend leaves him no alternative.

A later commentator on Sonnet 42, Miss M. M. Mahood, seems to be in general agreement with Knights regarding Shakespeare's witty indifference to or detachment from the whole affair. However, she obviously is more aware of the context provided by the preceding Sonnets, and her interpretation is fuller and more qualified:

> The dramatic irony of the plays . . . is matched in the sonnet by the irony with which Shakespeare contemplates himself excusing the inexcusable, and which is conveyed by the wordplay upon *excuse* and *approve. Excuse,* besides meaning 'make excuses, even where there is no justification for them' has the ironically impossible meaning of 'exculpate'; while if the youth *approves* the woman in the sexual sense, he can scarcely approve of her in the moral one. The incompatibility of these two sets of meanings explains as well as conveys Shakespeare's serene and witty detachment from the whole affair. The play on *excuse* shows that the youth's rivalry with Shakespeare's mistress troubles the poet far less than the sins of the spirit which he reproaches in more troubled sonnets, and the *approve* pun reflects Shakespeare's relief, after some anxiety, that the youth's behaviour is more wild-oat experimentation and that he is not wasting high feeling on a woman whom the poet knows by experience to be little worth it. Shakespeare has

71

understood the situation well enough to show his own role in it as a serio-comic one. No one could believe such fantastic rationalisations as are constructed here; Shakespeare himself mocks them, although he knows the unhappiness that constructs them.[45]

The play on "excuse" is obvious and fairly important; the alleged play on "approve" is unlikely, irrelevant, and probably imported from Sonnet 40 ("thou thyself deceivest / By wilful taste of what thyself refusest"). How these wordplays explain or even convey Shakespeare's serene and witty detachment will not be apparent to anyone who takes Sonnets 41 and 42 seriously and reads the whole group carefully. The first part of her statement about the "approve" pun—it "reflects Shakespeare's relief . . . that the youth's behaviour is mere wild-oat experimentation"—seems to be based on a casual and routine reading of Sonnet 41; the second part—"he is not wasting high feeling on a woman . . . little worth it"—apparently derives from a few lines of Sonnet 40 combined with reminiscences of the Dark Lady series. Her final sentence contains much that any critic would agree with, but the penultimate remark about Shakespeare's serio-comic role, a brief summary of her view of the Sonnet, is quite unacceptable.

III

Sonnets 57 and 58 concern a master-slave relationship in which the speaker plays the unhappy role of the slave of love, disliking his servile dependence and the bitterness of his friend's absence without being able to escape from emotional domination.[46] His resentment is realized by the sense, tone, and feeling of the Sonnets, by an obvious and bitter irony. Both Sonnets convey the misery of the true and watchful servant and in that respect may be a kind of expanded inversion of Luke 12:35–37:

> Let your loynes be girded about, and your lights burning,

And yee your selves like unto men that waite for their master, when hee will returne from the wedding, that when hee commeth and knocketh, they may open unto him immediately.

Blessed are those servants, whom the Lord when he commeth, shall finde waking: verely I say unto you, hee will girde himselfe about, and make them to sit downe at table, and will come forth, and serve them (Geneva Version, 1600).

In Sonnet 57 the implications of an initial generalization (in the form of a rhetorical question) are made clear by the particulars of succeeding lines, and the irony which is directed chiefly at his friend is also aimed at the poet himself.

> Being your slave, what should I do but tend
> Upon the hours and times of your desire?
> I have no precious time at all to spend,
> 4 Nor services to do, till you require.
> Nor dare I chide the world-without-end
>   hour
> Whilst I, my sovereign, watch the clock for
>   you,
> Nor think the bitterness of absence sour
> 8 When you have bid your servant once adieu.
> Nor dare I question with my jealious
>   thought
> Where you may be, or your affairs suppose,
> But, like a sad slave, stay and think of
>   nought
> 12 Save where you are how happy you make
>   those.
>   So true a fool is love that in your will,
>   Though you do anything, he thinks no ill.

He begins by asking a question needing no answer: As your abject inferior, subservient to your will, what ought I to do except be (always) ready to serve you whenever you want something (whenever you are through satisfying your appetites, your other needs and

73

longings that have nothing to do with me)? In fact, he continues, I have no time to spend that seems valuable (to me), and no services to perform for you until you ask or demand them. (I would like to have the opportunity to do the things for you that *my* loving friendship prompts me to, but you avoid me until you have some demand to make and thus cause me to waste a great deal of my time.) [47]

"The hours and times of your desire," built on a formula that is a hallmark of Shakespeare's style,[48] is deliberately ambiguous, enabling the poet to refer to different aspects of the same situation. It obviously points to the friend's demands on the speaker, with "desire" (wish, request, demand) looking forward to "require," and "hours and times" implying the few hours and occasions on which friendship is served. And despite the silence of the commentators, it also calls attention to the friend's neglect of the poet. In this sense the phrase is equivalent to "your times of pleasure" in Sonnet 58; "desire" (sensual appetite, lust) anticipates "will," and "hours and times" refers to the "world-without-end" hours and many occasions devoted to the pursuit of pleasure.

The irony of the second quatrain, which bears out my reading of "hours and times" and lines 3–4, is straightforward: I dare not curse the tedium of waiting for you, my lord and master, or even think that your absence is bitter. The striking compound in the phrase "the world-without-end hour" (l. 5), used by Shakespeare in only one other place, may remind one of the phrase "world without end" which occurs in the *Gloria Patri* and the hymn *Te Deum Laudamus* of the Book of Common Prayer,[49] as well as in Isaiah 45:17:

> Glory be to the Father, and to the Sonne: and to the holy Ghost
>
> As it was in the beginning, is nowe, and ever shal be: world without end.

We magnifie thee day by day,
  and world withouten end:
Adore thy holy name, O Lord
  vouchsafe us to defend
From sinne this day, have mercy Lord,
  have mercy on us all:
And on us as we trust in thee,
  Lord let thy mercy fall.

But Israel shall be saved in the Lord, with an ever-
lasting salvation: yee shall not be ashamed nor
confounded, world without ende.[50]
Perhaps one or more of these familiar passages suggested the phrase as a vivid means of conveying ever-
lastingness, the psychological truth that when we are
waiting for someone to come or for something to happen,
with all our attention and energy directed toward that
moment, even an hour seems endless. Here as in *Love's
Labor's Lost* (V.ii.797) Shakespeare thinks of love as
"a world-without-end bargain," and, because it is, the
enslaved speaker cannot hope that he "shall not be
ashamed nor confounded world without ende."

With the last quatrain the speaker's irony returns
more forcibly upon himself. He says, I dare not consider
too carefully with my justifiably suspicious mind where
you may be, or form too clear an idea of your affairs, for
your sake as well as my own; instead, like a sorrowful
and serious slave I wait for your return and think of
nothing except how happy you make those who are with
you—wherever you are. He cannot help thinking of
what his friend is doing—indeed, in a general way he
knows—but to preserve his self-respect he dare not inquire too closely.

Ambiguous in syntax and diction, the couplet summarizes his view of his slavery. There are at least three
ways of taking it: (a) So true a fool is love that in your
Will (the poet) / Though you do anything, he thinks

75

no ill; (b) So true a fool is love that, though you do anything, he thinks no ill in your will; (c) So true a fool is love that, though you do anything in your will, he thinks no ill. Since all these readings are consonant with the poem as a whole, there is no need of favoring any one of them to the exclusion of the others. The Quarto's "Will" invites us to regard it as the poet's name or a play on his name in the manner of Sonnets 135 and 136, "Whoever hath her wish, thou hast thy Will," and "If thy soul check thee that I come so near"; so faithful and genuine a fool is love that in the person of your friend Will he thinks there is no harm in whatever you do. In the second meaning of the line the constant fool who is the loving speaker thinks the friend's *intentions* are good, or rather not bad, whatever he does. This may also be a way of uttering a hoary commonplace by way of an excuse—that the volitional faculty itself is alway directed at what seems to be the good.

> The will, because of an instinct implanted in it by God, desires the good and abhors the evil which the reason represents to it. The will is sometimes called the rational appetite because it desires the good just as the sensitive affections desire the pleasing, and it abhors the evil just as they abhor the displeasing.[51]

According to the third reading, so loyal a fool is love that whatever the friend does that lies within his power of choosing, or in his willfulness or perversity, in his lust, the speaker thinks there is no evil in it.[52]

Setting aside the significance of "fool" for the moment, it is clear that "true" denotes loyal, constant, faithful, as well as real or genuine. Neither sense can be dispensed with, for although the speaker intends the phrase to convey strong self-reproach (So big a fool am I), the fool's loyalty to his friend is the basis of their relationship. Playing on the poet's name, "will" has all these senses: the volitional part of the rational soul, the power of choosing and willing; choice, wish, pleasure, desire; intention; willfulness or perversity; lust. Both "anything" and "he" are emphatic, and "ill" signifies (moral) evil, sin; harm, injury. There is an implicit disparity between what he, as opposed to others, thinks of his friend's intentions and actions. As a true fool he may see no personal injury, no sin against friendship, in them, but others who can see things objectively probably regard them as both morally evil and injurious to the speaker.

Here and elsewhere in the Sonnets the fool is one who has been made a fool of (by Love or Time), who is somebody's or something's dupe or sport: "Love's not Time's fool" (116); "the fools of Time" (124); "Thou blind fool, Love, what dost thou to mine eyes / That they behold and see not what they see?" (137). On the most obvious level, then, the speaker qualifies as a fool because he is stupid enough to be duped by love, which is traditionally blind. He is also a servant or slave, a talker, and a condoner of sin, roles which further entitle him to be called "fool." In relation to his sovereign he is something like a court fool—a privileged familiar who can say almost anything but is nevertheless a mere servant. Much as he dislikes his situation, as a slave he can only think and talk about it, complain at length but take no action. In this respect he is a talker (rather than a doer), and to talk is characteristic of the fool, as both etymology and the Bible suggest. "Fool" derives from a Latin word for bellows which in late Latin became windbag, fool; and a number of passages in Proverbs and Ecclesiastes remind us that "a fool . . . is full of words." In the Bible "fool" often signifies sinner, a sense that fits the poet to the extent that he sins in condoning ill, corrupting himself by salving the friend's amiss:

> To connive and wink at your friend's weaknesses, to gloss them over and to be taken in by them, even to admire and love his worst faults as if they were virtues—doesn't this look like folly? [53]

Yet in the final analysis perhaps it is the friend who is

the fool and the speaker who is wise, for in the Socratic view to know you are a fool is a sign of wisdom.[54]

Pooler describes the equivocal Sonnet 58 as a "complaint in the form of an assertion that he has no right to complain"; Empson agrees that it is "two-faced in idea." [55]

> That god forbid that made me first your
>   slave
> I should in thought control your times of
>   pleasure,
> Or at your hand th' account of hours to
>   crave,
> 4 Being your vassal bound to stay your leisure!
> O, let me suffer (being at your beck)
> Th' imprisoned absence of your liberty;
> And patience, tame to sufferance, bide each
>   check
> 8 Without accusing you of injury.
> Be where you list; your charter is so strong
> That you yourself may privilege your time
> To what you will; to you it doth belong
> 12 Yourself to pardon of self-doing crime.
>   I am to wait, though waiting so be hell;
>   Not blame your pleasure, be it ill or well.

It opens with a statement put in an ironic, almost sarcastic, optative mood: may the god (of love) that first made me your slave forbid that I should, *even in thought,* control the occasions of your pleasure, the times devoted to enjoyment, amusement, gratification (whether sensuous or sensual), to doing whatever you want to do; or that I should beg for an accounting of how you spend your time, for I am only your servant, obliged to wait till you are unoccupied.

The ironic optative continues in the second quatrain, which apparently stresses the poet's patient servility while it reveals a painful awareness of his grievances. He says, Since I am at your command, let me bear with patience and constancy the pain of the imprisoning ab-

78

sence resulting from your freedom and libertinism; [56] and may my patience, submissive to suffering and pain, endure each rebuke or taunt without accusing you of wrong or insult. Four words in these lines ("suffer," "patience," "sufferance," and "bide") [57] combine the notions of experiencing something which causes pain and grief and putting up with, making the best of it. The ostensible emphasis is on toleration, a necessary condition of slavery, but the speaker's sense of injury is equally prominent. Of course the friend has the liberty to be absent, the freedom to do what he wishes, even if absence imprisons the poet by keeping him from his friend. Yet if the friend flaunts his liberty by devoting his absences to libertinism, then it is natural for the speaker to feel wronged ("check," "injury," "crime"). "Check" signifies taunt as well as rebuke or reproof, and, in view of the implications of "pleasure" and "liberty," it probably glances at the term from falconry meaning to stoop for baser game and the baser game itself.[58]

In the third quatrain the friend's rights, already recognized in the references to liberty and pleasure, temporarily come to the fore. The poet says, be where you please; do what you want with your time; forgive yourself for any sin you commit and any injury you do to yourself. As "list" and "will" look backward (and forward) to "pleasure," so "charter" and "privilege" look back to "liberty," [59] for the senses of "liberty" include franchise, privilege, right, as well as freedom and libertinism. "Charter," signifying right or privilege, may also suggest a contract between them, a contract favoring the friend [60] because the speaker's love is so great. Indeed, it is the depth of the poet's love even more than the friend's character that makes one a fool and a slave and gives the other the prerogatives of a king.

The summarizing couplet states the requisites of the poet's position as he derives them from his experience: he is to wait and suffer and to suffer in silence. He must wait, even if it is a veritable hell of anxiety and misery to do so; he must not find fault with the friend's choice, with the gratification, whether good or bad, that keeps the friend from him even though it may be a rebuke or an insult. "Wait" has three senses which sum up the speaker's role with marvelous economy—to wait for, to keep watch, to be on duty or ready to serve; for he is at once the anxious loving friend, the ineffectual observer-guardian of his friend's behavior ("For thee watch I whilst thou dost wake elsewhere, / From me far off, with others all too near"),[61] and his friend's willing (and unwilling) servant.

4

This Vile World:
SONNETS 66, 121, AND 129

> Give me leave
> To speak my mind, and I will through and through
> Cleanse the foul body of th' infected world,
> If they will patiently receive my medicine.
> > *As You Like It*

> Most of the obvious emotions in words . . . are moral,
> marking approval or disapproval only, and it is a regular
> mark of moral feelings that they claim not to be private
> ones.
> > William Empson, *The Structure of Complex Words*

> There does seem to be some ground for believing that
> Hamlet, in his recoil from the grossness of physical ex-
> istence and his desire for death, expresses feelings that
> were personal to Shakespeare and not merely dramatically
> conceived. If this is so it may help to explain why the
> "negative" verse expressing loathing and recoil is, on the
> whole, so much more forceful than the passages in which
> any positive values are indicated.
> > L. C. Knights, "Prince Hamlet"

HOWEVER MUCH one may quarrel with the Knights
comment on Hamlet, and I would question his use of
"personal" and "explain," the point about the power of
the negative verse is well taken and is equally appropriate to the Sonnets. It is my conviction that many of
the finer poems of the collection are those which convey

81

negative feelings, whether mixed or relatively pure, and it is partially on this basis that I have selected Sonnets for discussion. In certain specialized forms this view seems to be rather widely held, many critics, for example, stressing the merits of Sonnets attacking devouring Time and dealing with death and mutability; [1] but the general tendency is to emphasize a few isolated Sonnets or those of a certain class to the exclusion of others that are as good or better. The Sonnets I now wish to consider, presenting their strong negative feelings chiefly in the form of moral indignation, are in no danger of being neglected or underrated.

Sonnet 66, as E. H. Wilkins pointed out long ago, has the three essential features of the Provençal *enueg:* " 'the list, the initial repetition, and the emphatic presence of a word denoting "annoyance." ' " [2] Consisting of one long sentence whose parallel clauses are all general and often figurative, this deceptively simple Sonnet presents a catalogue of reigning evils which makes it a powerful and perennial text for the times. From the standpoint of the speaker the poem might be called a death wish with reasons appended.

> Tired with all these, for restful death I cry:
> As, to behold desert a beggar born,
> And needy nothing trimmed in jollity,
> 4 And purest faith unhappily forsworn,
> And gilded honor shamefully misplaced,
> And maiden virtue rudely strumpeted,
> And right perfection wrongfully disgraced,
> 8 And strength by limping sway disablèd,
> And art made tongue-tied by authority,
> And folly (doctor-like) controlling skill,
> And simple truth miscalled simplicity,
> 12 And captive good attending captain ill—
> Tired with all these, from these would I be gone,
> Save that, to die, I leave my love alone.

The opening words signify more than emotional exhaustion, the weariness of frustration. In view of the Sonnet's feeling and tone, "Tired with all these" tells us that the poet is fed up, disgusted with all of the evils which follow, and thus longs for death to bring rest and oblivion. He sees "desert," men who are deserving by virtue of their natural equipment, their fine qualities, born poor and humble, forced to beg favors,[3] while those who are intellectually and spiritually less than nothing ("needy nothing") enjoy exceptional prosperity and have the euphoric insolence which often accompanies it. As Aristotle says in the *Rhetoric* (1391a),

> The wealthy are insolent and arrogant, being mentally affected by the acquisition of wealth, for they seem to think that they possess all good things. . . . They are luxurious and swaggerers. . . . In a word, the character of the rich man is that of a fool favored by fortune.

On the strength of the need and supplication suggested by his crying for death,[4] one may be inclined to include the speaker among the worthy beggars. "Trimmed," denoting dressed, furnished, arrayed, is both literal and figurative because of the meaning of "jollity," which refers not only to exceptional prosperity but also, in its more specific senses, to finery, splendor; insolent presumption or self-confidence; pleasure. After this sharp contrast between the poor and suppliant man of talent and the affluent, arrogant nonentity, between the gifts of Nature and those of Fortune, a moral or intellectual antithesis is implied in every line of the list.

The next four lines (4–7) are symmetrical in construction: a valued substantive is followed by a destructive verb, with each preceded by a modifier. "Faith" may signify fidelity, loyalty (to a person, cause, ideal); vow or pledged word; true love; (religious) belief; and "unhappily" is to be taken in its worst, most negative sense, for in the words of the homily "Against Swearing and Perjury," whoever "forsaketh the truth, for love or displeasure of any man, or for lucre and profit to him-

self, doth forsake Christ, and with Judas betray him."
Faith forsworn for love is exemplified by the speaker
and person addressed in Sonnet 152, "In loving thee
thou know'st I am forsworn"; faith forsworn for fear of
official displeasure and for profit, by many of the Cath-
olics who took the oath required by the Supremacy Act
of 1559, and by Bacon's prosecution of his friend and
patron Essex.[5]

The poet sees positions and titles of distinction put
in the wrong hands, given to those who are utterly un-
worthy of them.

> Let none presume
> To wear an undeserved dignity.
> O! that estates, degrees, and offices
> Were not deriv'd corruptly, and that clear
>   honour
> Were purchas'd by the merit of the wearer.
> How many then should cover that stand
>   bare;
> How many be commanded that command.[6]

He also sees pure virtue brutally, ruthlessly prostituted
and true perfection of person and character unjustly
disparaged and disfigured. "Maiden" and "strumpeted"
are both literal and figurative, since virtue as integrity
or moral goodness may be sacrificed for the sake of rank,
wealth, or power, and virtue as chastity may be de-
bauched through seduction, rape, or forced marriage.
Arranging marriages or even sexual liaisons for money
and advancement was apparently standard practice in
court circles to judge from a passage in Wyatt's satire,
"A Spending Hand":

> In this also se you be not Idell:
> Thy nece, thy cosyn, thy sister or thy
>   doghter
> If she be faire, if handsom be her myddell,
> Yf thy better hath her love besoght her,
> Avaunce his cause and he shall help thy
>   nede.

It is but love: turn it to a lawghter.
But ware, I say, so gold the helpe and spede,
  That in this case thow be not so unwise
  As Pandare was in suche a like dede;
Ffor he, the ffooll, of conscience was so nyse
  That he no gayn would have for all his
    payne.[7]

"Perfection" refers to excellence, whether physical or
moral or both, and "disgraced" has several relevant
senses: discredited; disparaged; put out of or dismissed
from (royal) favor; disfigured.[8] Each of these senses
could represent a stage in a courtier's decline and fall
in Shakespeare's day. To be discredited could result in
dismissal from royal favor, which in turn could result in
disfigurement through beheading or hanging—as in the
case of Essex and five of his fellow conspirators. In fact,
anyone who aroused governmental suspicion or dislike
on religious or political grounds ran the risk of being
disfigured by routine judicial torture.

Strength, like each of the qualities in the four preceding lines, is turned into its opposite; art is silenced by
those in power; with an air of wisdom ignorant stupidity controls expertise; unswerving loyalty is wrongly
called stupidity or foolishness; and, worst of all, good is
the helpless slave of triumphant evil. "Strength" denotes
power or resources which may be of various kinds—
physical, moral, intellectual, political, or military. It is
incapacitated, crippled, because the central control is
crippled or feeble; it is like a great country with an in-
competent, indecisive government or a seasoned army
with poor or misguided leadership.[9] Antony is a fine
case in point, a great ruler and soldier who "gives his
potent regiment to a trull," whose conduct of the war
with Caesar is such that "his whole action grows / Not
in the power on't. So our leader's led, / And we are
women's men" (*Antony and Cleopatra*, III.vii.68–70).

Censorship in general may well be deplored in line 9,
not simply censoring of plays and literary works, for

85

"art" signifies any skill resulting from knowledge (and practice), learning as well as professional or technical proficiency. The relevant meaning of "skill" is probably comprehended under "art." One may be tempted to distinguish between them on the grounds that art is weighted toward the acquired and theoretical while skill is weighted toward the native and practical, and yet "doctor-like" (in the manner of a Ph.D.) suggests that skill refers to fields of knowledge or expertness in which one can be a doctor rather than to those like poetry, drama, statecraft.[10] "Skill" could also have the general sense intelligence, judgment, discrimination, in which case the line would have a double meaning.

"Simple," which plays on the sense foolish or silly, means pure, unadulterated, unmixed; single-minded, as it does in Sonnet 125 ("For compound sweet forgoing simple savor"). Such simple truth is actually simplicity in the best sense,

> While others fish with craft for great opinion,
> I with great truth catch mere simplicity;
> Whilst some with cunning gild their copper
>   crowns,
> With truth and plainness I do wear mine
>   bare.
> Fear not my truth; the moral of my wit
> Is plain, and true; there's all the reach of it [11]

but to certain people or in certain circumstances it seems to be only foolishness:

> The loyalty well held to fools does make
> Our faith mere folly; yet he that can endure
> To follow with allegiance a fall'n lord,
> Does conquer him that did his master
>   conquer,
> And earns a place i' the story.[12]

The last line of the series is the terrible climax, conveying in one figure the complete reversal of the natural moral order. After such a harsh enumeration of the evils of this world, of the disparity between what is and what

86

should be, the couplet may seem like a weak anticlimax, but it is designed to manifest the strength of the poet's love. He would be glad to die were it not that by dying he would leave his love alone; thus it is love that imposes on him the disagreeable duty of living so that his friend [13] will not be left alone in this infected world.[14]

II

Although Sonnet 121, "'Tis better to be vile than vile esteemed," may be independent, it may also serve as a kind of generalizing conclusion to a group of poems beginning with Sonnet 109, "O, never say that I was false of heart," and consisting of small clusters of closely related Sonnets (109–112, 113–114, 115–116, and 117–120).[15] The general subject of this provisional group is the speaker's temporary transgression against friendship, an offense which includes moral sin and which was caused by, or resulted in, prolonged absence from his friend. He freely admits his errors,[16] but insists that these "worse essays" prove the friend his "best of love," that his love has been renewed and strengthened by his divagation:

> O benefit of ill! Now I find true
> That better is by evil still made better;
> And ruined love, when it is built anew,
> Grows fairer than at first, more strong, far
>   greater.
> So I return rebuked to my content,
> And gain by ills thrice more than I have
>   spent.   (Sonnet 119, ll. 9–14)

None of the Sonnets in this group seems to have a direct bearing on the interpretation of Sonnet 121. The only other Sonnet to deal with reputation is 112, and its sense, tone, and feeling are almost opposite to those of Sonnet 121: [17]

> Your love and pity doth th' impression fill
> Which vulgar scandal stamped upon my
>   brow;

For what care I who calls me well or ill,
4 So you o'ergreen my bad, my good allow?
You are my all the world, and I must strive
To know my shames and praises from your
   tongue;
None else to me, nor I to none alive,
8 That my steeled sense or changes right or
   wrong.
In so profound abysm I throw all care
Of others' voices that my adder's sense
To critic and to flatterer stoppèd are.
12 Mark how with my neglect I do dispense:
You are so strongly in my purpose bred
That all the world besides methinks are
   dead.[18]

However, these poems do remind us of something that
should be fairly obvious in Sonnet 121: though he is
indignant about his vilification, the speaker is not claiming complete innocence.

According to one group of commentators, Sonnet 121
is an indignant protest against Puritan attacks on the
stage, an angry defense of Shakespeare's profession.[19]
Others, with better reason, feel that it is aimed not "at
the Puritans, but at 'the world,' which puts the worst
possible construction upon conduct." [20] Still a third general view of the poem is represented by G. Wilson
Knight's remark that it asserts "some kind of beyond-
good-and-evil claim" [21] and by L. C. Knights's brief
comment:

> Sonnet 121, which has caused a good deal of per-
> plexity, seems to me mainly a protest against any
> rigidly imposed moral scheme, a protest on behalf
> of a morality based on the nature of the writer. But
> that morality can only be discussed in terms that
> poetry supplies.[22]

There is, of course, something to be said for all these
summary views, especially the second and the third, but

88

any critic must stand or fall on his interpretation of the details of this difficult Sonnet.

'Tis better to be vile than vile esteemed
When not to be receives reproach of being,
And the just pleasure lost, which is so
    deemed
4 Not by our feeling but by others' seeing.
For why should others' false adulterate eyes
Give salutation to my sportive blood?
Or on my frailties why are frailer spies,
8 Which in their wills count bad what I think
    good?
No, I am that I am; and they that level
At my abuses reckon up their own.
I may be straight though they themselves be
    bevel;
12 By their rank thoughts my deeds must not
    be shown,
    Unless this general evil they maintain—
    All men are bad and in their badness
    reign.

A sense of personal outrage underlies the main point of the first quatrain—to have an evil reputation that is undeserved is worse than being evil.[23] The sense of the quatrain, or rather of lines 3–4, is open to several interpretations, of which the simplest and perhaps easiest to arrive at is the following: It is better to be evil than to be judged evil when we receive this disgrace without deserving it and even lose, by not experiencing or feeling it, what is considered to be the appropriate or rightful pleasure in the view of others who slander us. This reading, which is similar to Tucker's, is guided by the natural syntax of the third and fourth lines. "Which is so deemed" is taken with "just pleasure," and "so," doing its common job of representing a word or phrase previously used, stands for either "just pleasure" or "just" or "pleasure" alone.

Another interpretation of the third and fourth lines regards "so deemed" as referring to "vile" and the pleasure as (a) being experienced but lost through condemnation, or (b) not experienced. Dowden and Wyndham offer the (a) version of this reading, G. Wilson Knight and perhaps Beeching the (b) version. Dowden glosses the lines as follows: "And the legitimate pleasure lost, which is deemed vile, not by us who experience it, but by others who look on and condemn." [24] Knight paraphrases them thus: "As it is, I merely lose the corresponding pleasure, which anyway only appears evil from an objective and impersonal viewpoint, and would not necessarily be felt as such, inwardly, by me." [25] Since the syntax of the Sonnets is often rather flexible or even free, this general view does not necessarily violate the syntax of the quatrain and it does receive some support from the community of meaning of "deemed" and "esteemed" (judged, considered, held).

A third interpretation of lines 3 and 4 depends on taking "just pleasure" as equivalent to "the pleasure of being just" (Schmidt) or as an elliptical reference to rectitude, good conscience, or good repute. This general view is represented by the comments of Tyler,[26] Pooler, Case, and Tucker Brooke. In his note on these lines Pooler asks,

> Can this mean: And when we lose the pleasure of being just [or the legitimate pleasure of having a good character] which is deemed a pleasure not so much from what we feel ourselves as from the way in which others regard us? For slander deprives a man of the second of the two natural rewards of virtue, *viz.* a good conscience and public approbation.[27]

Of course there is ample grammatical precedent for regarding "just pleasure" as a condensed form of "the pleasure of being just." [28] (For example, compare "the slow offense"—offense of slowness—in Sonnet 51; here, however, the descriptive meaning of the poem requires that the phrase be so construed, while in Sonnet 121 it does not.) Furthermore, one may argue that on a broad, relative definition of justice this general reading of the third and fourth lines fits the Sonnet as a whole as well as the quatrain. But I suggest that it entails at least an odd way of talking about justice if not an odd view of it. For, granting Shakespeare's concern with reputation as an index of worth, and the existence of some classical and Renaissance precedents,[29] how can the *pleasure* of being (relatively) just depend upon the opinion of others; or, to put it in Pooler's terms, how can slander deprive a man of the pleasure of a good conscience?

One may summarize the merits of the three main interpretations of lines 3–4 by saying that although all three fit both the quatrain and the Sonnet as a whole, the first and second fit better. Of these, the first is preferable because it depends on natural syntax and eliminates repetition in the second quatrain.[30]

The second quatrain consists of two rhetorical questions in which the speaker indignantly asks why his imperfections should be noted and exaggerated by those who are worse than he is. For why should the inconstant and falsifying adulterate eyes of others salute my (admittedly) amorous blood; despite my passionate nature,[31] why should slanderous adulterers greet me as an equal? Or why are my moral weaknesses spied on by people even weaker than I who arbitrarily judge bad what I think is good? "Give salutation to" must mean to salute or greet (as an equal or companion in sin), with a sense close to that of "salute" in *Troilus and Cressida* (III.iii.107–108), "eye to eye oppos'd / Salutes each other with each other's form," rather than in *Henry VIII* (II.iii.102–103), "Would I had no being, / If this salute my blood a jot." [32] Since it follows "sportive" (amorous or lustful), one assumes that prominent among the moral weaknesses of all kinds to which "frailties" refers is an inclination to sexual sport (cf. *Othello,* IV.iii.99 ff.). Taken generally, "in their wills" signifies wilfully or arbitrarily; in terms of the specific contrast between their wills and the speaker's, it also means desires (and inclinations), what they want as opposed to what the speaker wants. Doubtless one should want something because it seems good, but here something is good or bad according to whether or not one wants it. This is a case where Hamlet's statement applies: "there is nothing either good or bad, but thinking makes it so." [33] The spies, though morally worse than the speaker, are presumably frail in a different way, and hence they misunderstand and judge him harshly and crudely. However, the difference may work both ways, for he may be calling them "frailer" by virtue of their difference and not simply because they are rather hypocritical slanderers. At any rate, the quatrain apparently presents two contrasted slanders or misjudgments by those who are worse than the speaker: inconstant adulterers think that, being amorous, he is as sexually corrupt as they are; those with different moral weaknesses think him bad because different.

Something of a Petrarchan break occurs with the ninth line when Shakespeare asserts his openness and independence in words found in Exodus 3:14: "I am that I am." This may be a shorthand way of saying that to honest men he is what he seems, no better or no worse, with evident frailties but not vile or evil; that in his character, unlike Iago's, there is no difference between appearance and reality:

> For when my outward action doth demonstrate
> The native act and figure of my heart
> In compliment extern, 'tis not long after
> But I will wear my heart upon my sleeve
> For daws to peck at: I am not what I am. [34]

A more obvious gloss on the assertion is Wyatt's repetitious poem of self-defense, a partial analogue to Sonnet 121:

I am as I am and so wil I be,
But how that I am none knoith trulie,
Be yt evill, be yt well, be I bonde, be I fre,
I am as I am and so will I be.

I lede my life indifferentelye,
I meane no thing but honestelie,
And thoughe folkis judge full dyverslye,
I am as I am and so will I dye.

I do not reioyse nor yet complaine,
Bothe mirthe and sadnes I doo refraine,
Ande use the meane sins folkes woll frayne,
Yet I am as I am be it pleasure or payne . . .

And from this minde I will not flee;
But to you all that misiuge me
I do proteste as ye maye see
That I am as I am and so will I bee.[35]

The Biblical context of "I am that I am" leads some
readers to see it as a proud declaration of absolute freedom in which Shakespeare announces that, like God, he
is a law unto himself or, in Wilson Knight's phrase,
"beyond good and evil." If it is a kind of declaration of
independence, it is also moderate and relative, perhaps
no more than the condensed equivalent of, I know what
I am far better than my slanderers do, and my standards
are different from and probably higher than theirs,
hence their accusations are irrelevant and unwarranted.
And, he continues, those who aim at my faults or sins
are, by that very act of guessing at or attacking them,
enumerating their own, for "filths savour but themselves." I may be comparatively upright though they be
crooked themselves. My doings ought not to be put before the public by their foul thoughts, are not accurately
presented by such a corrupt medium—unless they assert

and can support this generalization about evil (or, evil generalization): all men are bad and in their badness reign.

"Level at" signifies to aim or direct (a weapon) at, which in turn gives rise to the senses to guess at or conjecture; to attack. In lines 9–10 Shakespeare seems to have only a general basis for his charge that to attack his sins is to reveal one's own—after all, to the pure all things are pure; he is not necessarily claiming that "they" commit the same sins. His position here is closer to Matthew 7:1–2 ("Iudge not, that ye be not iudged. / For with what iudgment ye iudge, yee shall be judged, and with what measure ye mete, it shall be measured to you againe") than to Romans 2:1 ("Therefore thou art inexcusable, O man, whosoever thou art that iudgest: for in that that thou iudgest another, thou condemnest thy selfe: for thou that iudgest, doest the same things"). "Maintain" in the couplet must denote defend, support; vindicate, as well as assert as right or true, in order to fit the syntax of lines 12–13 and to emphasize the untenability of the concluding proposition.

The last line is difficult to gloss or paraphrase, chiefly because of the unusual use of "reign." Among the various definitions that have been proposed for "reign" are "exult in, be made happy by" (Schmidt), "to go on or continue *in* some state or course of action" (Pooler), and "persist?" (Ridley).[36] Tucker offers this gloss for the whole line: "'*all* men are bad, and are prevailingly so in *their* particular form of badness.' Thus if a man is licentious, he thinks licentiousness is the 'reigning' vice" (p. 199). Possibly the use of "reign" here is due to the influence of Biblical contexts:

> For if by the offence of one death reigned through one, much more shall they which receive aboundance of grace, and of the gift of righteousnes, raigne in life through one, Jesus Christ.
>
> That as sinne had raigned unto death, so might

grace also raigne by righteousnesse unto eternall life, through Jesus Christ our Lord.

Let not sinne reigne therefore in your mortal body, that yee should obey it in the lusts thereof.

(Romans 5:17, 21; 6:12)

Actually, the obvious general senses of "reign" (to rule or govern; to be predominant, to prevail) may be adequate to the pessimistic view which is being summarized and rejected. It is an ancient commonplace that the world was made for man, who rules the world because he is God's noblest creation (v. *Comedy of Errors*, II.i. 20 ff.). Ralegh puts it this way near the beginning of his *History of the World* (1614):

Man, thus compounded and formed by God, was an abstract or model, or brief Story in the Universal: in whom God concluded the Creation, and work of the World, and whom he made the last, and most excellent of his Creatures, being internally endued with a divine understanding, by which he might contemplate, and serve his Creatour, after whose Image he was formed, and endued with the powers and faculties of Reason and other abilities, that thereby also he might govern and rule the World, and all other God's Creatures therein.[37]

I suggest that Shakespeare's general intention in the last line of Sonnet 121 is to present the preposterous antithesis of this traditional view of man's nature and his place in the universe. Instead of reigning by virtue of his excellence, whether actual or potential, man rules the world in and by his badness. Since it is unthinkable that the poet's slanderers could actually maintain such a generalization, it serves to destroy the case against him by reducing their position to the absurd. Despite the bitterness of Sonnet 66, there is no place in Shakespeare's range of values for the kind of cynicism that Elizabethans associated with the realistic Machiavelli: "whoever desires to found a state and give it laws, must start with assuming that all men are bad and ever ready to display their vicious nature, whenever they may find occasion for it." [38]

III

The celebrated Sonnet 129, "Th' expense of spirit in a waste of shame," is inevitably compared to passages in *Venus and Adonis* (1593) and *The Rape of Lucrece* (1594), which also deal with lust by means of simple rhetorical devices. In *Venus and Adonis* (ll. 799–804) Shakespeare is content to define the inadequacy of lust in terms of simple antithetical comparisons, partly in the interests of decorum, for "the text is old, the orator too green":

> Love comforteth like sunshine after rain,
> But Lust's effect is tempest after sun;
> Love's gentle spring doth always fresh
>   remain,
> Lust's winter comes ere summer half be
>   done.
>   Love surfeits not, Lust like a glutton dies;
>   Love is all truth, Lust full of forged lies.

In *Lucrece* (ll. 694–714) he moralizes at greater length and more elaborately (full simile followed by exclamation with detailed allegory) on appetite, surfeit, and revulsion.

> Look! as the full-fed hound or gorged hawk,
> Unapt for tender smell or speedy flight,
> Make slow pursuit, or altogether balk
> The prey wherein by nature they delight;
> So surfeit-taking Tarquin fares this night:
>   His taste delicious, in digestion souring,
>   Devours his will, that liv'd by foul
>   devouring.
>
> O! deeper sin than bottomless conceit
> Can comprehend in still imagination;

Drunken Desire must vomit his receipt,
Ere he can see his own abomination.
While Lust is in his pride, no exclamation
    Can curb his heat, or rein his rash desire,
    Till like a jade Self-will himself doth tire.

And then with lank and lean discolour'd
        cheek,
With heavy eye, knit brow, and strengthless
        pace,
Feeble Desire, all recreant, poor, and meek,
Like to a bankrupt beggar wails his case:
The flesh being proud, Desire doth fight
        with Grace,
    For there it revels; and when that decays,
    The guilty rebel for remission prays.

Since the passage occurs after Tarquin's rape of Lucrece, each stanza naturally dwells on post-coital surfeit and revulsion, but each ends with a contrast between lust before and after satisfaction. The predatory
cruelty of lust is implicit in the simile of the first stanza
and is stressed by the concluding traductio ("Devours
. . . devouring"). Its moral blindness is remarked in
the next stanza's first four lines (an excellent gloss to
the couplet of Sonnet 129), its wild willfulness in the
last three lines. The third stanza presents an allegorical
description of depleted Desire who, having fought with
Grace before vomiting his receipt, now begs for forgiveness. Desire's physical appearance is designed to realize —
that loss of vitality which according to Renaissance
physiology resulted from sexual relations, especially
when excessive, and which is referred to in the first line
of Sonnet 129. Sperm, it was believed, is made from
blood, a large amount of which is transformed into a
small amount of seed. Consequently, "the loss of seed
'harmeth a man more, then if hee should bleed forty
times as much.' 'And this is the cause why such as use
immoderate *Venus*, be short lived, and as the Sparowes,

97

through incontinencie consume themselves.'"[39] Like a
man drained of energy by intercourse, Desire is generally feeble and drowsy ("With heavy eye"), with a face
that is thin, shrunken ("lank"), and bloodless ("discolour'd").

‑From the standpoint of its rhetoric Sonnet 129 is perhaps as simple as, if not simpler than, the passages from
the narrative poems. The Sonnet might be described as
consisting of variations on a theme,[40] employing rhetorical figures of repetition and variation (traductio,
anaphora, chiasmus) and antithesis to secure its effects.
To be more precise, the method of lines 5–12 might be
called incremental variation, a gradual advancement
and development of the meaning through differences—
sometimes comparatively slight—in the words and
phrases of successive lines. There are relatively few
comparisons in the poem, and it lacks the balanced
regularity of the stanza from *Venus and Adonis* and the
formal elaboration, the fine medieval technique, of the
Lucrece stanzas. But it achieves far greater intensity of
feeling, with its impassioned statement rising to a crescendo in the middle sections and declining to a resigned conclusion:

> Th' expense of spirit in a waste of shame
> Is lust in action; and, till action, lust
> Is perjured, murd'rous, bloody, full of blame,
> 4 Savage, extreme, rude, cruel, not to trust;
> Enjoyed no sooner but despisèd straight;
> Past reason hunted, and no sooner had,
> Past reason hated, as a swallowed bait
> 8 On purpose laid to make the taker mad;
> Mad in pursuit, and in possession so;
> Had, having, and in quest to have, extreme;
> A bliss in proof—and proved, a very woe;
> 12 Before, a joy proposed; behind, a dream.
> All this the world well knows; yet none
> knows well

To shun the heaven that leads men to this
  hell.[41]

Perhaps the best way to approach this famous poem is to consider first the senses and implications of some of its words and phrases. In the first line, "expense" denotes expenditure, consumption; waste; loss, "waste of shame" is equivalent to shameful waste, and "spirit" is a technical term from Renaissance physiology. On its most specific level "spirit" probably signifies the vital spirit(s) which carries the natural heat and moisture of the blood; "sexual indulgence consumes blood and spirit," robbing one of the heat and moisture essential to life.[42] Donne makes this clear in the following lines:

     freely on his she friends
He blood, and spirit, pith, and marrow
  spends,
 Ill steward of himself, himselfe in three
  yeares ends.[43]

Another, more general sense of "spirit" is obviously vital power or energy, and it seems to denote soul or mind also, if only because passions are faculties of the sensitive soul.

Lust in operation is a shameful waste of one's physical and spiritual substance, but until it is satisfied it deprives man of his humanity, reducing him to the level of an animal. "A man once given over to his lust . . . is no better than a *beast*," says Burton.[44] Thus in the list of pejoratives of lines 3–4, exemplifying the figure asyndeton, "murd'rous," "bloody," "savage," "rude," and "cruel," all of which overlap in sense, emphasize the predatory, single-minded animality of the lustful man. "Extreme" is also significant in this respect, for lust is not only the extreme or highest degree of desire, and hence excessive, totally unrestrained, but it also pushes man to one extreme or limit of his nature, making him pure animal. It does this, of course, by subjecting man's highest "soul," the rational, to his sensitive soul, by subjecting reason to passion. The sensitive soul, which perceives external objects as either pleasant or unpleasant and directs the body in obtaining or avoiding them, is the highest soul of animals. "Bloody" refers to lust's willingness to shed blood, whether by deflowering or killing, to attain its object, as well as to its being "of" the blood: "Lust is but a bloody fire" (*Merry Wives of Windsor*, V.v.101). In this second sense, consisting of blood, it fits both the preliminary and final stages of lust, applying to lust as sexual tumescence and reminding us that for the Renaissance a mere abundance of healthy blood makes one amorous. "Perjured," one of the few words in the list which could not be used of an animal, signifies that lust thrives on broken vows and deliberate lies. Under the influence of lust, men will not hesitate to break an old marriage vow or to promise undying love for the sake of a casual liaison. (v. *A Lover's Complaint*). As Burton says, "the more effectually to move others, and satisfy their lust, they will swear and lie, promise, protest, forge, counterfeit, brag, bribe, flatter and dissemble of all sides," [45] a point which he supports by his customary array of examples.

According to the grammar and Quarto punctuation of lines 1–8, "lust" is the subject of this long sentence. However, with the fifth line the subject under discussion becomes lust's object, action, or satisfaction; for it is not lust itself which is no sooner *enjoyed* than despised, past reason *hunted* and then hated, but rather the partner-victim and the culminating act, though doubtless the resulting loathing also comprehends lust. The fifth line is expanded by lines 6–8 for purposes of realization, especially in lines 7–8 which realize the ensuing revulsion. "No sooner had" restates and almost repeats "Enjoyed no sooner," for here the specific sense of "had" is equivalent to that of "enjoyed": sexually used or possessed (said of a woman). "Despisèd straight" is restated and expanded by "Past reason hated, as a swallowed bait . . . ," a clause which reminds us that the basic comparison in the quatrain is that of lust to an animal hunting food and being deceived by poisoned bait. Some of the implications of "Past reason hunted" are listed in preceding lines (3–4), and since "past" signifies beyond the reach or range of; outside the limit or sphere of, "past reason" might be defined briefly by "extreme" and "mad." Reason is the limit or natural boundary which is violated by extreme desire and extreme hatred. Besides vivifying post-coital revulsion, lines 7–8 also suggest its cause—the discrepancy between expectation and result. Anticipating the solid food of satisfaction, the lustful man only gets what later seems a swallowed bait (an enticement to feed) deliberately set out to make him mad. He blames the bait when he actually deceives himself; but there may also be, by a slight shift in focus, an underground attempt to lessen the burden of self-deception as the speaker considers the dangers of prostitutes, those baited traps which could through the pox make one literally mad.

In all modern editions of the Sonnets the ninth line of the Quarto, "Made in pursuit and in possession so," has been amended to "Mad in pursuit, and . . . ," an improvement which is quite unnecessary, for it hardly affects the sense and only makes the line a bit flatter by depriving it of an active verb. "Made" of the Quarto derives from "make" in the previous line, and "so," representing a word previously used, stands for "mad," hence the line is equivalent to made mad in pursuit and in possession. Riding and Graves, in their well-known attack on modern revision of the Quarto text of this Sonnet, offer a different view:

> the idea of *Mad* is only vaguely echoed in this line from the preceding line. The meaning of the line might reasonably be restricted to: 'Made In pursut and in possession as follows': since it is the first line of the sestet, it is more likely to refer forward than back. As a matter of fact, it does both.[46]

Here, as elsewhere in their essay, the authors seem to be swallowing a camel while straining at a gnat.[47] To accept their interpretation of "so" is to disrupt the sense of the quatrain, for if it signified "as follows" one would expect an enumeration of characteristics (cf. ll. 3–4) rather than what one does find—two pairs of parallel and relatively independent clauses.

Of course line 9, the first of the last quatrain, does refer forward to line 10 as well as back to line 8. The tenth line, summarizing the extremism of the lustful man before, during, and after satisfaction, parallels the ninth while adding another dimension. "In quest to have" restates "in pursuit," and both look back to "hunted," "having" restates "in possession," and "extreme" replaces "mad" understood; "had," looking back to lines 6–7 and forward to lines 11–12, has no counterpart in the preceding line. Incidentally, with line 9 the subject of discourse apparently has shifted to the taker of the bait; in line 11 it shifts back to action again. Riding and Graves take the opposite view: "It must be kept in mind throughout that words qualifying the lust-business refer interchangeably to the taker (the man who lusts), the bait (the object of lust) and lust in the abstract."[48] Granted that Shakespeare may well be thinking of all the elements of the lust situation throughout, his diction (not grammar or punctuation) makes it clear that he focuses his attention upon one or another in various parts of the poem.

To return to the quatrain, the eleventh line stresses the differences, amid general similarities, between stages of action, an extreme delight while experienced ("in proof"), an extreme grief afterwards. (Shakespeare has not "been at pains to show all along that lust is all things at all times," as Riding and Graves assert.[49] On the contrary, he has pointed out that it is only certain things at all times, namely, "mad" and "extreme.") This line, like others, has connections with what goes before as well as what comes after; for example, "in proof" is related to "having" and "proved" to "had." Line 12, also falling into antithetical halves, parallels line 11 and advances the sense of the quatrain. Among the senses of "proposed" are set before one's mind—as a goal or reward; anticipated; imagined; while some of the implications of "dream" are suggested by *Lucrece* (ll. 211–212): "What win I if I gain the thing I seek? / A dream, a breath, a froth of fleeting joy." The pleasure of action is insubstantial and fleeting, "momentany as a sound, / Swift as a shadow, short as any dream,/ Brief as the lightning in the collied night" (*Midsummer-Night's Dream*, I.i.143–145). For Riding and Graves "the final meaning of the line" is,

> Even when consummated, lust still stands before an unconsummated joy, a proposed joy, and proposed not as a joy possible of consummation but one only to be desired through the dream by which lust leads itself on, the dream behind which this proposed joy, this love, seems to be.[50]

This is simply the result of dragging in by the ears the implicit contrast between lust and love, even though Shakespeare's chief concern in this Sonnet is to define and deplore lust itself. They go on to note that this "ultimate" meaning is "inlaid with other meanings" which "should follow naturally" from it and which are all "possible and legitimate"; but of the readings they list, only one (the third) seems more than remotely possible.

In many of the Sonnets the couplet either summarizes the sense of what has just been said or introduces a qualification, alternative, or contradiction beginning with "but" or "yet." Although the couplet here may seem to combine both functions, it only refers to the sense of the quatrains in summary fashion and then contradicts and qualifies itself. "All this the world well knows" points to what has been said and admits that it is a tissue of commonplaces. "Yet none knows well" may be read in two ways, one of which is submerged or secondary. Taking line 13 in isolation, a step encouraged by the text of the Quarto, the phrase completes and contradicts the first part of the line by emphatic use of chiasmus—"All this the world *well knows* yet none *knows well.*" This interpretation, however, is overridden by the sense and syntax demanded by the last line, so that everything after "yet" qualifies the opening of the couplet:

> All this the world well knows; yet none
> knows well
> To shun the heaven that leads men to this
> hell.[51]

The main senses of "knows" are is aware of, understands and knows how to; "heaven" probably refers to woman and the pleasures of sexual relations ("I'll make my heaven in a lady's lap" [*III Henry VI*, III.ii. 148]),[52] "hell" to the extreme and generally painful emotional stress involved (cf. Sonnet 58, l. 13), with perhaps a glance at hell as the locus of sexual enjoyment (cf. Sonnet 144, l. 12). In a general way everyone is well aware of what lust is, if only from what religion and traditional morality have to say about it; yet one does not know it really well on this basis, does not know how to escape those occasions of sin which lead to its emotional hell. No one knows what lust is until he has experienced it, and we are all subject to lust.

> O! deeper sin than bottomless conceit
> Can comprehend in still imagination;
> Drunken Desire must vomit his receipt,
> Ere he can see his own abomination.

5

Constancy to an Ideal Object:
SONNETS 123, 124, AND 125

A man who has truly loved, though he may come to recognize the thousand incidental illusions into which love
may have led him, will not recant its essential faith. He
will keep his sense for the ideal and his power to worship.

A friend's only gift is himself, and friendship is not friendship, is not a form of free or liberal society, if it does not
terminate in an ideal possession, in an object loved for its
own sake. Such objects can be ideas only, not forces, for
forces are subterranean and instrumental things, having
only such value as they borrow from their ulterior effects
and manifestations. To praise the utility of friendship . . .
is to lose one's moral bearings.

George Santayana, *Reason in Society*

SONNETS 123, 124, and 125 are all related, each defining
in a different way some essential quality of the speaker's
love for the person addressed in Sonnet 125, each ending with a solemn assurance of the speaker's truth and
troth. Sonnet 123, which looks back to Sonnet 122, is the
simplest and least interesting of the group, consisting
of an extended defiance of Time and change and a vow
to be true despite them. In Sonnet 124, the most difficult
of these three poems, the speaker asserts that his love is
not subject to such agents of change as Time, Fortune,
or Policy. And Sonnet 125, the most interesting of this
group and one of the finest poems of the entire collec-

tion, presents the only basis on which friendship can exist in the speaker's true soul.

Sonnet 123 is addressed to Time, the chief abstraction-adversary of the Sonnets because

> beauty, wit,
> High birth, vigour of bone, desert in service
> Love, friendship, charity, are subjects all
> To envious and calumniating time.
>
> (*Troilus and Cressida*, III.iii.171–174)

A challenge to Time's sovereignty is hurled in the opening line, a challenge which is justified by the quatrains and restated more lucidly in the couplet.

> No, Time, thou shalt not boast that I do
>   change!
> Thy pyramids built up with newer might
> To me are nothing novel, nothing strange;
> 4 They are but dressings of a former sight.
> Our dates are brief, and therefore we admire
> What thou dost foist upon us that is old,
> And rather make them born to our desire
> 8 Than think that we before have heard them
>   told.
> Thy registers and thee I both defy,
> Not wond'ring at the present nor the past;
> For thy records and what we see doth lie,
> 12 Made more or less by thy continual haste.
> This I do vow, and this shall ever be—
> I will be true, despite thy scythe and thee.

The first quatrain is open to at least three different interpretations, one of which takes the reference to the "pyramids built up with newer might" as specific and historical, while the others take it as general and symbolic. Within the quatrain itself "built up with newer might" and "dressings of a former sight" lend support to the first view, quite apart from any contemporary achievement of archaeological reconstruction or restoration. However, the most recent exponent of this view, Leslie Hotson,[1] finds such an achievement in the erection of a huge Egyptian obelisk each year from 1586 through 1589 by Pope Sixtus V.[2] With these structures in mind, and knowing that to the Elizabethans the meaning of "pyramids" included *"slim spires,* and particularly *obelisks,"* Hotson offers the following "comprehensible summary" of the first quatrain and the second:

> Standing firm himself, the poet scorns the tricks of Time. He declines to join the childish world in its admiration over a nine days' wonder which it regards as a "strange novelty." Everybody's talking about the pryamids brought forth—as if produced for their special delight—from the womb of earth by the autocrat of Rome and his engineer. The poet is not impressed. After all, these obelisks, while newly set up, consecrated, and dressed with his armorial bearings and Christian crosses by Sixtus, are in fact no new invention, but some 3000 years old, and we have heard about them from historians. Though now palmed off as a novelty on an ignorant wo:ld gaping for curiosities, their austere shafts, bearing Time's registers in royal hieroglyphs, were common sights ages ago.[3]

Of course, if one is committed to a topical interpretation of the Sonnet, other structures erected at a different time and place may seem more suitable. Alfred Harbage, for example, believes it is more probable that the poem alludes to pyramids set up in London in 1603 to welcome King James.[4]

A second, more common reading of the first quatrain, represented by the views of Beeching, Knights, Pooler, and Wilson Knight, regards the pyramids as standing for any imposing modern structure designed to be relatively permanent. To the speaker, the recent attempts to produce enduring monuments are not at all novel or surprising. He knows that this sort of thing has been done before, that these pyramids are imitations and variations ("dressings") of earlier monuments, and hence like everything but the human soul they belong to Time ("Thy pyramids"). This interpretation, the simplest and most accessible, is neatly summarized by L. C. Knights's first paraphrase of the first quatrain:

> Time cannot make his boast that I change with his passage. The admired wonders of modern architecture are not novelties to me (since my conscious self is, in a sense, outside time); I have seen them all before, and I know that the modern examples are only variations on the old.[5]

"Strange" has the obvious senses new; unknown; remarkable, surprising,[6] but "dressings" may be glossed in various ways: "trimming up, refashioning" (Onions), "rehabilitations" (Lee), "representations, dressings-up" (Tyler), and so on. I suggest that its general sense is disclosed by comparison with "dressing old words new" in Sonnet 76 (l. 11),[7] its specific sense by the meaning of the French word from which it derives, *dresser* (to arrange; to erect, set up, raise; to fashion; to build or make).[8]

In an effort to point out the ambiguity of the first two quatrains, Knights offers a second paraphrase of this quatrain which purports to be the equivalent of Wyndham's interpretation:

> Time cannot boast that I change. The pyramids—built with a skill that was new compared with my age-old self [with newer might to me]—were, I saw, no novelties even in Egypt but merely dressings of a former sight.[9]

This is a good attempt to clarify Wyndham's reading,[10] which is far from the plain sailing he thought it was, but the phrase in brackets indicates that it puts a severe strain on the syntax of lines 2–3 (in the manner of Riding and Graves).

Still another interpretation of the first quatrain is set forth by Tucker, who reads the whole poem in terms of Sonnets 124 and 125. A surface meaning resembling the second general view of the quatrain, and perhaps including an allusion to the completion of St. Peter's at Rome, is dismissed as "but a figure of speech," while the following reading is offered instead:

> The poet is thinking of the new personalities who are towering into prominence beyond his now waning friend, and concerning whom other writers are building ambitious poems of praise. For both the word and the notion cf. Drayton *Past.* 4. 6 'He that the world's pyramids would build / On those great heroes . . . / Should have a pen, etc.' [11]

The main difficulty here is that, although "pyramids" may suggest new pillars of society, new holders of power and influence, such a meaning seems rather peripheral. To judge from the rest of the poem, the pyramids are supposed to be the work of masonry, gilded monuments of some sort. Furthermore, the Drayton passage cited looks like an example of the familiar claim that the pen is mightier than the pyramid (compare Sonnet 55 and Whitney's emblem, *Scripta manent*).[12] It is hard to see how it could be relevant here when the speaker is concerned with asserting the constancy or stability of the loving soul as opposed to the mutability of matter, rather than with praising or eternizing a "waning friend." [13]

Of these four chief interpretations of lines 2–4, the second seems most acceptable because it best fits the Sonnet as a whole as well as the generality of reference in the quatrain. An historical, literal reading is also quite possible, though it is obviously impossible to say just what Shakespeare had in mind—it may have been Roman obelisks, or St. Peter's, or some other striking monument. In any case, to interpret these lines literally should not affect their general implications. Of the other two readings, Tucker's is of some value in calling attention to certain undercurrents of the poem, but Wyndham's is merely an eccentric variation on the literal view.

As far as the second quatrain is concerned, there is fairly general agreement about the sense of lines 5–6. Most of those who paraphrase these lines as well as those who gloss only a few words would accept Knights's rendering: "Man's life is short; therefore he tends to wonder at things, foisted upon him by Time as novelties, which are really old. . . ."[14] "Dates" signifies lives; "admire" means wonder at; admire, and "foist" refers to palming or passing off something as other than it is. Most of the commentators who concur on the general sense of lines 5–6 also concur on that of lines 7–8, although they may differ slightly in their glossing of the eighth line. Perhaps the two best readings of this line are Tyler's—"And prefer to regard them as really new, just 'born' "—and Pooler's—"think them the novelties we wish to see." To represent the majority view of these lines I choose Dowden's gloss rather than the remainder of Knights's paraphrase of the quatrain simply because Dowden's is fuller:

"Them" refers to "*what* thou dost foist," etc.; we choose rather to think such things new, and specially created for our satisfaction, than, as they really are, old things of which we have already heard.[15]

Wyndham disagrees with this general interpretation of lines 7–8 on grounds of grammar and sense:

Assuming these lines to refer to 'what' Time 'foists upon us,' the second implies that we ought to recognise the old things foisted upon us by Time for objects previously known, but that we 'prefer to regard them as really new' . . . (Tyler), and 'specially created for our satisfaction' (Dowden). The explanation is not satisfactory, though probably the best to be got from the assumed reference. But (1) this reference of 'them' to 'what,' followed by a singular 'that is,' can hardly be sustained grammatically, and (2) it scarce makes sense. Shakespeare cannot have intended that we admire things for their age while 'we regard them as really new.' I suggest that the plural 'them' refers grammatically to the plural 'dates,' and that the word usually printed 'born' in line 7, had best be printed 'borne' as it is in the Quarto (= *'bourn'*). We make our brief dates into a bourn or limit to our desire (*cf.* 'confined doom,' CVII.4) instead of recollecting that 'we have heard them told' (= *reckoned*) 'before.' [16]

Although much could and should be said against them, Wyndham's comments have been received in silence, except by L. C. Knights, who combines them with Wyndham's remarks on the first quatrain to make up a second reading of lines 1–8.[17] In the first place, Wyndham's objection to the prevalent view of lines 7–8 rests on a misreading of lines 5–6, or at least a distortion of the commonest interpretation of them. Neither Dowden nor Tyler said or implied that "we admire things for their age while 'we regard them as really new' "; quite the opposite. But Wyndham himself is compelled to accept this "admiration for age" distortion in order to adjust lines 5–6 to his own unlikely reading of the first quatrain. Furthermore, as far as syntax and grammar are concerned, syntax supports the reference of "them" to "what thou dost foist," and Shakespearean and Elizabethan grammar can provide thousands of examples of the agreement of apparently singular with plural forms. Nevertheless, I agree that line 7 may signify that we make our brief lives into a limit to our desire—this is one implication of the Sonnet as a whole and the basic reason for Knights's acceptance of Wyndham's interpretation; but we are still faced with the problem of working in his reading of line 8, which as it stands "scarce makes sense." [18]

In order to understand more fully the intentions and implications of the first two quatrains it is useful to consider them in the light of two famous passages. The first is from Ecclesiastes (1:9–11), the second from *Troilus and Cressida* (III.iii.175–180):

What is it that hath bene? that that shall be: and what is it that hath bene done? that which shall be done: and there is no new thing under the sunne.

Is there anything, whereof one may say, Behold this, it is newe? It hath bene already in the olde time that was before us.

There is no memorie of the former, neither shall there bee a remembrance of the latter that shal be, with them that shall come after.

One touch of nature makes the whole world kin,
That all with one consent praise new-born gawds,
Though they are made and moulded of things past,
And give to dust that is a little gilt
More laud than gilt o'er-dusted.
The present eye praises the present object.

What the first quatrain makes clear is that the speaker has the knowledge, without the world-weariness, of the preacher in Ecclesiastes. He knows that there is nothing new under the sun, that generation succeeds generation while only earth and time abide forever. The second quatrain, despite the inclusive "we," brings his consciousness of change into contrast with the relative blindness of others, a blindness which is also defined by the lines from *Troilus*. All men have a natural trait (and taint) which makes them love apparent novelty; thus they are taken in by Time's latest gawds, though they are only the old made new. Our liking for the new stems from the brevity of our lives in two respects: "the present eye praises the present object," and, more important, we fear destructive change and what reminds us of it. But the speaker can accept and defy mutability because, as he points out in the last six lines of the Sonnet, he knows its powers and limits.

He defies both Time, the measure of present change, and the registers that record the past, being surprised at neither past nor present, since "wonder is the effect of ignorance." [19] For the records and memorials of the past as well as what we see in the present (such as the pyramids) deceive us, give us a false sense of values, in that Time's swift passage makes them either more or less than they are. What has already been said (ll. 1–8) emphasizes that what Time brings forth in the present is generally magnified (in importance and novelty); what it leaves behind in the past is generally diminished. But change cannot affect the essential self, the human soul, and hence the speaker can confidently vow that despite Time he will keep his "constancy in plight and youth, / Outliving beauty's outward, with a mind / That doth renew swifter than blood decays" (*Troilus and Cressida*, III.ii.168–170).[20]

II

Sonnet 124, in some respects a complex continuation of 123, is perhaps the most difficult of all the Sonnets to interpret in detail. Although its general drift and intention are fairly clear, nearly every word, phrase, and line admits of at least two different interpretations, a fact which makes for a large and varied mass of commentary. Instead of attempting to impose some kind of order on this critical chaos, I shall confine myself mainly to the presentation of my own views, with only an occasional glance at the readings of others. But before I begin to wrestle with the text, I should like to quote Tucker's admirable headnote on the poem, and perhaps the best way to approach it:

> Though the general purport of the piece is clear— viz. that the poet's love does not vary with the circumstances of the beloved—its individual expressions and their connections have perplexed every reader. In many cases the commentator has hampered himself with preconceptions as to the identity of the friend, and has endeavoured to force his interpretation to the circumstances of Essex or Southhampton. The proper procedure is to seek the coherent sense which should be yielded by the language itself, and to leave any individual

application—if one is to be attempted at all—
until that task is accomplished. In point of fact
the poem contains nothing to point to any particular individual or circumstances.[21]

Tucker's general statements about the Sonnet seem
quite just on a preliminary reading.

> If my dear love were but the child of state,
> It might for Fortune's bastard be unfathered,
> As subject to Time's love or to Time's hate,
> 4 Weeds among weeds, or flowers with flowers
>   gathered.
> No, it was builded far from accident;
> It suffers not in smiling pomp, nor falls
> Under the blow of thrallèd discontent,
> 8 Whereto th' inviting time our fashion calls.
> It fears not Policy, that heretic
> Which works on leases of short-numb'red
>   hours,
> But all alone stands hugely politic,
> 12 That it nor grows with heat nor drowns with
>   show'rs.
> To this I witness call the fools of Time,
> Which die for goodness, who have lived
>   for crime.

Since the first quatrain is put into the subjunctive, it
is evident that the speaker is setting up a contrary-to-
fact straw man to tear down in succeeding quatrains.
Yet though we are well aware before we reach the
pivotal "No" [22] that the speaker's love is not the "child
of state" or subject to Time or Fortune, the implications
of the quatrain represent not so much a fruitless excur-
sion into the realm of "as if" as negative definition or
realization. In the opening line "dear" signifies valuable
or precious, "love" refers to the feeling rather than the
person loved, and "state" has relevant senses which are
variously touched on in the remainder of the poem.
"State" here (as opposed to "state" in Sonnet 29,
"When, in disgrace with Fortune and men's eyes") in-

cludes all those externals that are separable from a person's self or character—status, rank, wealth, ceremony, power, authority—things which are the gifts of Fortune or the rewards of policy (the art of acquiring them).[23] In Sonnet 125, where the point is again made that the speaker's genuine love does not depend on such things, it is symbolized by the canopy (sometimes called a "state") which covers the chair of state:

> Were't aught to me I bore the canopy,
> With my extern the outward honor-
> ing . . . ?

Line 2 of Sonnet 124 suggests the extent to which "state" depends upon Fortune, the strumpet who is continually producing bastards, bringing some people into prosperity at the top of her wheel while plunging others into adversity at the bottom. A love which sprang from state,—external circumstances and the gifts of Fortune—would be always in danger of being deprived of its father or nominal object, or being disowned or disinherited because of some new object. (As Pooler says, "behind all the metaphors" of these opening lines "there seems to be the thought that if my love for my friend arose only from his prosperity, it would have no motive or ground of existence if his fortune changed.")[24] Line 3 may be taken in at least two different ways: (a) as explaining how the love of state might or might not be unfathered, and (b) as pointing out another hazard to which such a love would be subject. On the first reading the child of state would be unfathered if Time hated it but would not be if it were loved by Time. According to the second reading the speaker is asserting that the love of state is subject not only to Fortune but to Time, the obstetrician who delivers Fortune's bastards. Thus if his dear love were of this kind it would be just as "subject to Time's love or to Time's hate."[25] The fourth line, which has never been glossed satisfactorily, is extremely difficult. However, some of the difficulties may be overcome by assuming that the speaker is thinking of the child of state and Fortune's bastard rather than his dear love, hence the plural forms, and that the line is roughly parallel to the third. Often in Shakespeare weeds stand for what is worthless or bad (witness Sonnets 69 and 94) while flowers stand for what is valuable and good; but here they apparently represent adversity and prosperity, respectively. When Fortune's bastards and the children of state are loved by Time and flourishing, they are flowers; when they are hated by Time and in decline they are weeds; in either condition Time may gather them, cut them down.[26] Pooler puts it somewhat differently, "Strictly, 'weeds' may denote courtiers or public men neglected; 'flowers,' those in favor," [27] and cites *Richard II* (V.ii.46–47): "who are the violets now / That strew the green lap of the new come spring?"

With the second quatrain the speaker begins to characterize his own love more directly, but still chiefly by contrast to the inferior political kind he has just sketched. It has, unlike Time's pyramids in Sonnet 123, been builded far from "accident" (almost synonymous with "state") in the depths of the true soul. The next three lines expand the assertion of the fifth by describing certain accidents which have no effect on his love. It does not suffer in smiling pomp, nor does it perish under the blow of the thralled discontent to which the time tempts our fashion. "Accident" denotes "chance, fortune; whatever is not essential (because present by chance or fortune)" and probably has a slight metaphysical coloration. The fifth line as a whole may be designed to recall Matthew, 7:24–25:

> . . . I will liken him to a wise man, which hath builded his house on a rocke:
> And the raine fell, and the floods came, and the windes blewe, and beat upon that house, and it fell not: for it was grounded on a rocke.

In the sixth and seventh lines the speaker's love becomes a king reigning in serene stability, equally immune to the cares of pomp and the dangers of rebellion. "Suffers" probably means sustains injury, damage, or loss and, as the equivalent of "falls," be killed or destroyed; perish. "Pomp," one aspect of state, signifies splendor, magnificence; greatness, power; and Schmidt glosses "smiling pomp" as "the favour of greatness." Smiling pomp presumably stands for prosperity, while thralled discontent represents adversity; thus lines 6 and 7 look back to the fourth in a general way. Though it is possible for love to suffer even in the midst of prosperity, in line 6 Shakespeare is perhaps thinking more in terms of the vehicle of the metaphor than the tenor and along the lines of Henry V's famous soliloquy on ceremony:

> what art thou, thou idle ceremony?
> What kind of god art thou, that suffer'st
>   more
> Of mortal griefs than do thy worshippers?
> What are thy rents? what are thy comings-
>   in?
> O ceremony! show me but thy worth:
> What is thy soul of adoration?
> Art thou aught else but place, degree, and
>   form,
> Creating awe and fear in other men?
> Wherein thou art less happy, being fear'd,
> Than they in fearing.[28]

"Thrallèd discontent," the discontent of those who feel enslaved or enthralled, fits the tenor of the metaphor quite as well as it does the political vehicle.[29] Love or friendship can enslave a person and cause justified discontent—witness Sonnets 57 and 58—but here there is the suggestion that the times tempt the ordinary friend or lover to feel discontent on the grounds that loyalty to one person is a kind of slavery. According to the eighth line, which is hard to render idiomatically, the times tend to make discontent a habit or fashion. "Inviting" denotes tempting or enticing; "calls" has the obvious sense summons, invites; and "fashion" signifies customary mode of behavior; prevailing custom, conventional usage. Brooke glosses "our fashion" as "our fashionables, those who live the courtly life," and says that the *inviting time* predisposes them . . . to be discontented and restless." [30] This meaning of "fashion," though not recorded until the nineteenth century, certainly fits both the sense and intention of the quatrain.

In the third quatrain the speaker considers his love in relation to state as Policy, the government or management of public and private affairs. Policy is completely Machiavellian, for it is not only prudence in the management of affairs, a kind of selfish worldly wisdom, but also cunning, treachery, deceit, and intrigue. His true and enduring love does not fear Policy, which is a heretic because it has no faith or loyalty and takes the short selfish view. It works on leases of a few hours "like a tenant on a short lease who exhausts the land in his own immediate interests." [31] But his love stands all alone, self-sufficient and unique, towering above the world in its genuine wisdom, so that it neither increases in favorable, nor dies in unfavorable, circumstances. Knowing full well that "Love's not Time's fool" (Sonnet 116), he ends by calling upon the fools of Time to testify to the truth of all that he has said. This testimony is provided by their lives: they die in favor of goodness though they have lived for the sake of crime.

Regarding "politic" Tyler remarks that it "seems here equivalent to self-sufficing, desiring no increase or extension, and fearing no enemies, like a well-ordered city or state," [32] citing in support *Much Ado About Nothing* (V.ii.65–66): "so politic a state of evil that they will not admit any good part to intermingle with them." I would compare the whole eleventh line with these lines (21–22) from Donne's "The Sunne Rising": "She's all States, and all Princes, I, / Nothing else is." The twelfth line is probably parallel to lines 6–7, presenting another set of metaphors for adversity and prosperity. Each quatrain has its representative of these two extremes, and the relationship of lines 4 and 12 is based on the prosperity-adversity antithesis rather than on natural images (weeds and flowers are emblematic or symbolic). The figures of line 12 are intended to represent purely external conditions, fair weather and foul, and yet they also carry hints of inner weather; "grows with *heat*" suggests the temporary growth of interest under the influence of lust or desire, while "drowns with show'rs" suggests the death of love to the accompaniment of weeping.[33]

I take "this" in line 13 to refer to all that has preceded it, not merely the last quatrain; and the fools of Time, Time's dupes or sports, are either all people whose loves are the opposite of the speaker's or the loves themselves, the children of state doomed to brief lives. In the last line "for," often a tricky word in the Sonnets, has several possible meanings: in favor of; with the result of benefiting; for the sake of; for lack of (a common meaning) is ruled out by the intended antithesis between goodness and crime.[34] "Crime," frequently used in the general sense of sin or fault, refers to sins against love and loyalty, especially those implicit in the pursuit of state. The fools of Time have lived for (in favor of, for the sake of) their selfish and venal kind of love ("crime"); having learned by bitter experience how unsatisfactory it is, when they come to die they may well be in favor of the speaker's kind ("goodness").[35]

A final word on the Sonnet may be provided by a passage which is at once part analogue and part commentary, Jeremy Taylor's summary of the extremes and vicissitudes which true friendship must endure and overcome:

> . . . the proper significations are well represented in the old hieroglyphic, by which the ancients depicted friendship; "In the beauties and strength of a young man, bareheaded, rudely clothed, to signify its activity, and lastingness, readiness of action, and aptnesses to do service: upon the fringes of his garment was written 'Mors et vita,'

as signifying that in life and death the friendship was the same: on the forehead was written 'Summer and winter,' that is, prosperous and adverse accidents and states of life: the left arm and shoulder were bare and naked down to the heart,—to which the finger pointed, and there was written 'Longè et propè:' " by all which we know that friendship does good far and near, in summer and winter, in life and death, and knows no difference of state or accident, but by the variety of her services: and, therefore, ask no more to what we can be obliged by friendship; for it is everything than can be honest and prudent, useful and necessary.[36]

III

Sonnet 125 is a continuation of Sonnet 124 in the sense that once again the speaker's true unstinting love is contrasted with affection that depends on state, here equivalent to all outward displays of loyalty and devotion. The speaker rejects the devotion that manifests itself in forms and ceremonies, mere shows of service, in the rhetorical questions of the first two quatrains; in the last quatrain he offers his simple wholehearted love as the alternative.

> Were't aught to me I bore the canopy,
> With my extern the outward honoring,
> Or laid great bases for eternity,
> 4 Which proves more short than waste or ruining?
> Have I not seen dwellers on form and favor
> Lose all, and more, by paying too much rent,
> For compound sweet forgoing simple savor—
> 8 Pitiful thrivers, in their gazing spent?
> No, let me be obsequious in thy heart,
> And take thou my oblation, poor but free,
> Which is not mixed with seconds, knows no art

12   But mutual render, only me for thee.
          Hence, thou suborned informer! A true
              soul
          When most impeached stands least in thy
              control.

The disparity between these attachments is presumably
similar to the difference between the empty protestations of Goneril and Regan, who love state and not their
father, and the reticent love of Cordelia; between the
seeming friendship of Iago and the genuine devotion of
Desdemona; or between the loyal service Iago sneers at
and the following of self he practices:

          I follow him to serve my turn upon him;
          We cannot all be masters, nor all masters
          Cannot be truly follow'd. You shall mark
          Many a duteous and knee-crooking knave,
          That, doting on his own *obsequious* bond-
              age,
          Wears out his time, much like his master's
              ass,
          For nought but provender, and when he's
              old, cashier'd;
          Whip me such honest knaves. Others there
              are
          Who, trimm'd in *forms and visages* of duty,
          Keep yet their hearts attending on them-
              selves,
          And, throwing but shows of service on their
              lords,
          Do well thrive by them, and when they have
              lin'd their coats
          Do themselves homage: these fellows have
              some soul;
          And such a one do I profess myself. For, sir,
          It is as sure as you are Roderigo,
          Were I the Moor, I would not be Iago:
          In following him, I follow but myself;
          Heaven is my judge, not I for love and duty,

121

But seeming so, for my peculiar end:
For when my *outward* action doth demon-
strate
The native act and figure of my heart
In compliment *extern,* 'tis not long after
But I will wear my heart upon my sleeve
For daws to peck at: I am not what I am.[37]

With such a context in mind one is far less likely to dis-
tort the octave of the Sonnet than if one allows the
superficial connections of some of its words to guide
him.

The rhetorical question of the first quatrain is put
into the subjunctive mood to make it clear that the
speaker not only rejects the actions he describes but
also denies performing them. Would it mean anything to
me, he asks, if I "bore the canopy" of state, honoring
with my presence and outward action the externals
(appearance, rank, office, wealth) pertaining to you (or
another), or laid great hopes for the uncertain future on
the favor of great persons? There are many historical
examples from the sixteenth and seventeenth centuries
of the canopy of state being carried over kings, queens,
and other nobles during progresses and processions;[38]
here "bore the canopy" is clearly a general metaphor
that is expanded or explained in the second line. Many
readers take "*the* outward" to be the same as "*thy* outward" in Sonnet 69, where it refers mainly to physical
beauty. Although the outward may include a reference
to physical appearance, in this case it is subordinate to
those aspects of state, such as office and rank, which are
honored by state as pomp and ceremony. After all, the
canopy is carried over a king, for example, not because
of his beauty or fine character but solely because of his
rank and office. The conjunction of "outward" with line
3, especially "eternity," leads most commentators to
read lines 3–4 in much the same way as Dowden: "The
love of the earlier sonnets, which celebrated the beauty
of Shakespeare's friend, was to last for ever, and yet

it has been ruined." [39] The third and fourth lines *may* glance at the eternizing Sonnets, and Dowden's reading may be one way of accounting for the apparent recollection of the assertion in Sonnet 124 that his love was "builded far from accident." Nevertheless, if I understand the grammar of the quatrain correctly, this interpretation is based on nothing more substantial than a stock response, for the speaker claims he did *not* do the things he talks about. I suggest that in view of the context and common Shakespearean idiom "great bases" is a condensed form of "bases in (or on) greatness," where "greatness" signifies those persons who are important by virtue of position, rank, wealth, power, and so on. The speaker might have laid his bases for eternity,[40] his hopes for prolonged success in the future, on the favor and influence of great ones. Such an eternity proves more short than waste or destruction partly because "what's past and what's to come is strew'd with husks / And formless ruin of oblivion" (*Troilus and Cressida*, IV.v.165–166), partly because the favors of "princes" are so uncertain:

> O! how wretched
> Is that poor man that hangs on princes'
> favours!
> There is, betwixt that smile we would aspire
> to,
> That sweet aspect of princes, and their ruin,
> More pangs and fears than wars or women
> have;
> And when he falls, he falls like Lucifer,
> Never to hope again.[41]

In the rhetorical question of the second quatrain the speaker gives one good reason for rejecting the course of action he has just described—the cost is often too great. Have I not seen, he asks, those who spend their lives in the forms and visages of duty lose all their former advantages and resources and more (their prospects and hopes, their self-respect and the respect of others, and even their lives) in paying too much outward service for what another owns and controls, for the sake of the sweet drug of sharing in state, forgoing the simple delight of genuine friendship or love, becoming nothing but miserable failures (even if apparently successful) who are exhausted in their gazing. "Dwellers on form and favor" is a rich phrase that may be read in at least two different ways, depending on how one understands "form and favor." As Beeching and several others interpret the phrase, "form" means figure or shape and "favor" signifies face; thus he glosses it as "admirers of beauty only in form and face." [42] This is certainly one meaning that the phrase may readily bear, but it is not the only meaning or the most general one. The dwellers are those who live, rely, depend, and spend time on something, who are exalters of and sticklers for it. [43] "Form" has much the same meaning that it has in Juliet's "Fain would I dwell on form" (*Romeo and Juliet*, II.ii.88): decorum, good manners; convention; outward ceremony or formality; and "favor" signifies aspect or appearance—especially social appearances; face or visage; the good will or kindness of one's superiors. In short, "form and favor," although it does include some more favorable implications, is equivalent to Iago's "forms and visages of duty." The sixth line reminds us, through its figure of one who pays more rent (for a show place) than he can afford, that dwelling on form and favor both is and entails a reprehensible and yet pathetic keeping up of appearances. For the follower or courtier must not only pay, at terrible cost to his soul, the rent of homage, flattery, and fear (v. *Henry V*, IV.i.263–271), but he must also dress and live in a style befitting his role and ambitions. The result of it all is not gain but loss—of money, time, security, respect, and hope; it all ends in nothing:

> Thirteen years your Highness's servant, but yet nothing. Twenty friends that though they say they will be sure, I find them sure too slow. A thousand

hopes, but all nothing. A hundred promises but yet nothing. Thus casting up an inventory of my friends, hopes, promises, and times, the sum total amounteth to just nothing. . . .

The last and the least, that if I be born to have nothing, I may have protection to pay nothing, which suit is like his, who having followed the court ten years, for recompense of his service commited a robbery, and took it out in a pardon.[44]

"Compound sweet" is also open to several interpretations, such as sweet compound (with "compound" referring to a compounded drug) or multiple sweetness; multiple or complex pleasure or gratification. The sweetness is multiple because lord and follower gratify each other, or because the suitor is sweet, pleasing and flattering, to more than one person and hence receives pleasure from more than one source. On this last reading of "compound sweet," which is supported by "seconds" in the third quatrain, lines 6–7 would mean that the pitiful thrivers lose everything by diffusing their efforts, by following too many great persons (at once), forgoing the gratification of loyal devotion to one for the sake of (possible) rewards from several.[45] "Savor" like "odor" stands for an inner moral quality, and "simple savor" is the "sweet odor" of Sonnet 54, the "simple truth" of Sonnet 66—plain, single-minded devotion or loyalty to one person. The eighth line epitomizes the plight of the dwellers on form and favor: all that these shallow followers have to offer is exhausted in and by the activity that typifies their function, gazing (the dwelling on the face and figure of their lord); hence they are pitiful thrivers, businessmen who are wretched and pitiable failures.[46]

The third quatrain, in a mixed imperative-optative mood, opens with a dramatic pivotal "No" as the speaker prepares to give his answer to the problem of the previous quatrains. His alternative conception of devotion is based on a humble and unselfish love, on love as

125

agapé (a stream of givings) rather than *eros* (a stream of gettings).[47] No, I cannot manifest my love in formal service, he says to his friend; let me be loving and dutiful in respect to your heart (rather than in your public presence), and please accept my offering of a devotion that is modest but fully and freely given, which is not adulterated by self-interest or by other (subordinate) attachments (second choices) and is not skilled in artifice, knows only the art of mutual surrender, change, and exchange: "me for thee." In the ninth line, looking back to the first, second, and fifth, "obsequious" denotes devoted, loving, dutiful, obedient, while glancing at the rejected sense slavish, fawning, and "heart" represents the essential qualities of character or soul as opposed to form and favor and the externals of state. "Oblation" (offering or sacrifice) confers the utmost seriousness on his love by virtue of overtones derived from its religious senses (a gift or offering to God; the Eucharist); indeed, the diction of lines 7, 10, and 11 recalls the language of the opening chapters of Leviticus (1:9, 13): "for it is a burnt offering, an oblation made by fire, for a sweet savour unto the Lord" (cf. Ephesians, 5:2). "Free" signifies that, however poor in show his offering may be, it is rich in pure affection. The syntax of lines 11–12 is rather ambiguous, but whether one accepts a modern text or that of the Quarto,
> Which is not mixt with seconds, knows no art,
> But mutuall render, onely me for thee,

has no great effect on their meaning, although the Quarto punctuation does make it clear that "art" means artifice or artificiality, cunning, as well as the art of mutual render. "Seconds," which may well recall "compound sweet"—in fact, lines 10–12 present the alternative to the second quatrain—is usually explained in Steevens' terms as a second grade of flour ("his offering shalbe of fine flour"—Leviticus 2:1), and his gloss "unmixed with baser matter" has been almost universally accepted.[48] Steevens' comment emphasizes the vehicle of the metaphor; Onions' definition, "inferior rivals," emphasizes the tenor and is a little closer to those secondary friends or patrons, entailing the baser matter of selfishness, to which "seconds" refers. The speaker's love is unadulterated, has no second choices in reserve, no second in rank standing "heir to th' first" [49] in case the first should fail. It only knows the rare art of mutual "render," the complete exchange, surrender, and change of mutual *agapé* which is here described as "only me for thee." [50]

The poem ends in one of the most violent couplets in all the Sonnets. With a harsh command the speaker dismisses the "suborned informer," then tells him why his efforts could never succeed. A suborned informer is one who has been bribed or induced to commit perjury, to bear false witness against another; to be impeached is to be disparaged or discredited, charged or accused of something. If one takes the informer to be a person rather than an abstraction, one may assume that he has been procured by self-interest, like the decipherers and informers Nashe speaks of, who put princes

> in fear where no fear is, and . . . make a hurly-burly in the realm upon had-I-wist, not so much for any zeal or love to their princes or tender care of their preservation, as to pick thanks and curry a little favour, that thereby they may lay the foundation to build a suit on, or cross some great enemy they have. . . .[51]

Whoever the informer so abruptly apostrophized may be, he is certainly not the friend addressed in the last quatrain. He may be Time, the villain of Sonnet 123 and one of the enemies in Sonnet 124; or, what is more likely, he may be Jealousy, who is called an "informer" in *Venus and Adonis*, in the only other Shakespearean passage in which this word appears:

> For where Love reigns, disturbing Jealousy
> Doth call himself Affection's sentinel;

127

Gives false alarms, suggesteth mutiny,
And in a peaceful hour doth cry "Kill, kill!"
Distempering gentle Love in his desire,
As air and water do abate the fire.

This sour informer, this bate-breeding
      spy . . .[52]

In any case, on the basis of the octave of the Sonnet one may suppose that the informer—whether Jealousy, or a person, or any distorted view of the speaker's devotion —has accused the speaker of not having a true soul because he scorns the forms and visages of duty (or because on some occasion he may have paid homage to another). But a soul that is truly constant has nothing to fear from the policy of an informer; thus when it is most strongly charged with disloyalty it is freest from his control.

6

Some Tentative Conclusions

In Shakespeare one sentence begets the next naturally; the meaning is all inwoven. He goes on kindling like a meteor through the dark atmosphere. . . .

Shakespeare's intellectual action is wholly unlike that of Ben Jonson or Beaumont and Fletcher. The latter see the totality of a sentence or passage, and then project it entire. Shakespeare goes on creating, and evolving B. out of A., and C. out of B., and so on, just as a serpent moves, which makes a fulcrum of its own body, and seems forever twisting and untwisting its own strength.

Coleridge, *Table Talk*

IF ONE is entitled to generalize only upon a demonstrated knowledge of all or most of the relevant particulars, then like everyone else who has written on the Sonnets I have no right to offer general conclusions. Yet here as in many aspects of criticism one must compromise between the ideal state of affairs and practical necessity. Although I have handled only slightly more than half of the Sonnets, surveying the interrelations of more than tweny-five and examining more than twenty others in some detail, I have reflected upon them all. In that case it may be fairly safe to offer a few generalizations about characteristics of the collection. I shall begin with the chief implications of my analyses of individual Sonnets and their relationships.

The Order of the Quarto

On the basis of my discussion of about a third of the Sonnets and my examination of all of them, I must conclude that the order of the Quarto is generally and essentially right and that the burden of proof rests on those who think otherwise. Such criteria as sense, grammar, imagery, rimes, catchwords, and rare words tend to support the following assertions: (a) Sonnets which fall together belong together; (b) connected Sonnets are in the proper sequence since nearly always each Sonnet grows out of its predecessor: in a linked group A-B-C, B will grow out of A and C out of B.[1] Sense, grammar, and catchwords are the best indications of connection or relation between Sonnets,[2] as I hope my analyses have made clear, but such minor features as rare words or rimes often provide additional, fairly objective evidence. For example, "humor" occurs only twice in the Sonnets, "mayst" three times, and each of them appears in the connected Sonnets 91 and 92; only in the related Sonnets 95 and 96 does "sport" occur. Furthermore, a study of rare words might well tend to substantiate the assumption that the order of the Quarto is correct for apparently *unrelated* as well as related Sonnets: note, for example, "o'ersways their power" (65), "strength . . . sway" and "beggar" (66), "beggared" (67); "rank" (121), "rank" and "record" (122), "records" (123); "render" (125), "render" (126).[3] In short, I am in general agreement with E. K. Chambers' view that

> there is no advantage to be gained by rearranging the order of the 1609 volume, even if there were any basis other than that of individual whim on which to do so. Many of the sonnets are obviously linked to those which follow or precede them; and although a few may conceivably be misplaced, the order as a whole does not jar against the sense of emotional continuity, which is the only possible test that can be applied.[4]

130

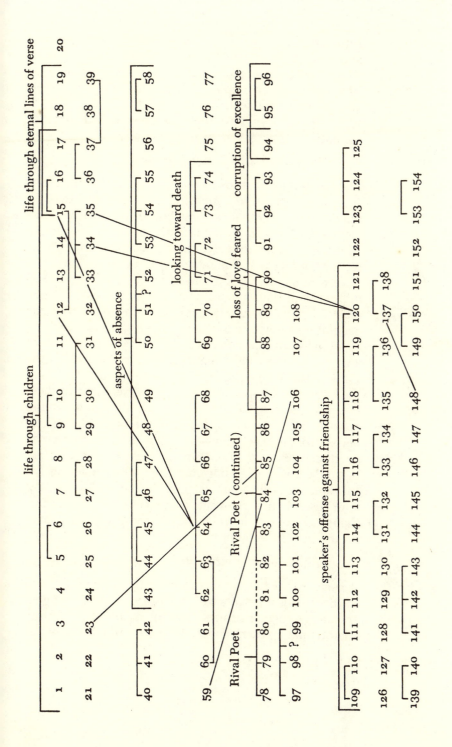

Although the sense of emotional continuity may be the only test that can be applied to the collection as a whole, there are others, as I have just pointed out and Chambers himself implies, which enable one to determine the interconnections of its parts. On the basis of such criteria I suggest that the Sonnets fall into the (tentative) groups shown in the chart.[5]

The Contexts of Interpretation

The inevitable result of the perception of interrelations and groupings in the Sonnets is that one reads them in the light of each other: a given Sonnet is compared with members of its group, with contiguous or more remote Sonnets, in order to arrive at its meaning. And rightly so, for the fact that Sonnets 33 and 34 are followed by 35 or that Sonnet 69 is followed by 70, makes a marked difference in their general meaning and in the way one must interpret them. Such relationships may affect the general meaning of a Sonnet (53 and 54), the meaning of a part—quatrain, couplet, line, phrase, or word (57 and 58), or the *total* meaning, the parts as well as the gross whole (93, 94, 95). This amounts to saying that the nature and importance of the interrelations of these poems varies considerably—a fact which is obvious and normal under the conditions that pertain in an Elizabethan sonnet collection—and that their character can be discerned only after careful comparative reading. It is also a way of reaffirming the point I made in the Introduction: the Sonnets provide for each other the most useful and relevant contexts of interpretation, though of course the relevance of the plays and longer poems cannot be ignored.[6]

The Kinds of Ambiguity

It is clear that the basic reason for the interrelations of the Sonnets is recurrence of similarity, especially of general and particular subjects and the means of presenting and organizing them. Since there are various degrees as well as kinds of similarity, it follows that there are also multiple relationships among the poems; and with the fact of multiple relationships goes the probability of some ambiguity, whether external or internal. If a Sonnet's relation to its context is not clear, if more than one Sonnet can be used as the context controlling interpretation (93 and 95 with 94), or one Sonnet can be used in different ways (70 with 69), then the reader is confronted by external ambiguity and the probability of a variety of general approaches and interpretations. Internal ambiguity, that of a part or parts of a Sonnet, may also be pointed up by the controlling context or contexts; witness the seventh line of Sonnet 94 when read in terms of Sonnets 93 and 95. However, such ambiguity is also a common feature of the individual or isolated Sonnet (129), since it is not only native to our analytic language but also was fostered by the flexible grammar and expanding vocabulary of Shakespeare's time.

In itself ambiguity is neither a merit nor a demerit; it is simply a neutral fact that must be accepted, if only because it is a natural feature of the English language. Its value in poetry depends upon the use to which it is put: it can be advantageously exploited, as it is in Sonnets 94, 57, and 58, or it can be mainly a kind of obstacle, as perhaps it is in Sonnet 124. But even where it makes for difficulties in interpretation it may also make for richness of meaning (94 and 40); as Richard Carew remarked, "Yea, soe significant are our wordes, that amongst them sundry single ones serve to expresse diuers thinges. . . ." [7] In any case the clarity and simplicity of much poetry is an illusion or delusion resulting from superficial reading.

Among the kinds of ambiguity that I have discussed or touched on are ambiguity of feeling, of syntax, of descriptive meaning of a part of the poem (word, phrase, line, quatrain, and so on). There is a fair amount of ambiguous syntax in the Sonnets, though probably less than Riding and Graves and Empson suppose,[8] while ambiguity of the word, phrase, or line is extremely common, partly because of the nature and state of the language, partly because of the character of Shakespeare's mind and his sensitivity to the resources of language. Shakespeare, like the rest of us, thinks and writes along lines largely determined by intraverbal associations: linguistic habit links words in many ways into complexes, and when any element of a complex or cluster occurs it makes the occurrence of some other element more probable.[9] In short, Shakespeare's verbal processes are not unique, but what is unique is his command of them, the freedom, ease, and frequency with which he makes significant verbal connections. This mastery of language is partially the result of his having "a wide rather than sharp focus to his mind" and his snatching "ideas almost at random from its balanced but multitudinous activity."[10] J. Dover Wilson is getting at the same point in a more traditional way when, with Johnson in mind, he says,

> Shakespeare habitually thought in quibbles, if indeed "quibble" be the right term for what was one of the main roots of his poetic expression. When he used a word, all possible meanings of it were commonly present to his mind, so that it was like a musical chord which might be resolved in whatever fashion or direction he pleased.[11]

Some of the words I have discussed illustrate Wilson's statement very well; note, for example, "soil" in Sonnet 69, "sense" (vs. "sensual") in Sonnet 35, "will" in Sonnet 57, "watch" (vs. "wake") in Sonnet 61, and "state" in Sonnet 124. In most of these cases Shakespeare's associative mind is exemplified by the word play; other cases will illustrate the re-creation of word and image that T. S. Eliot has commented on:

> The re-creation of word and image which happens fitfully in the poetry of such a poet as Coleridge happens almost incessantly with Shakespeare. Again and again, in his use of a word, he will give

134

a new meaning or extract a latent one; again and again the right imagery, saturated while it lay in the depths of Shakespeare's memory, will rise like Anadyomene from the sea. In Shakespeare's poetry this reborn image or word will have its rational use and justification; in much good poetry the organisation will not reach to so rational a level.[12]

A striking and large-scale manifestation of what Eliot is talking about, of the associative powers of Shakespeare's mind, is the shifting imagery of Sonnet 125. A unified poem with what some readers feel is a bewildering assortment of metaphors, Sonnet 125 is often regarded as the classic example of the variety of imagery to be found in some of the Sonnets, and of Shakespeare's tendency to rush from metaphor to metaphor instead of organizing his poems through a controlling image (in the manner of Sidney or Donne).[13] To a reader like Ransom this amounts to a failure to commit "the feelings in the case . . . to their determination within . . . [an] elected figure," a failure in (poetic) logic, at least to the extent of taking "lines of least resistance." [14] Yvor Winters would doubtless regard the poem as typical of the "unbalance which distinguishes the Shakespeare of the sonnets . . . most sharply from his great contemporaries, . . . Jonson, Greville, Donne, and even Sidney," an unbalance which occurs "wherever the poet's sensibility to the connotation of language overbalances his awareness of the importance of denotation." [15] Even careful students and warm admirers of the Sonnets are apt to think that, despite the excellence of Sonnet 125, it exhibits a disturbing inconsistency of imagery. In reply to these various doubts and damnations one can only point out that the method of Shakespeare (in a given poem) is not the method of Sidney or Jonson or Donne; that there is more than one poetically valid way of developing a general subject; and that "in the lyric, where the associative process is strongest and the ready-made descriptive phrases of ordinary prose furthest

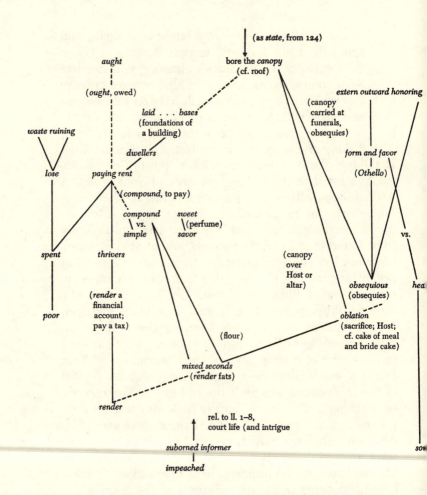

away, the unexpected or violent metaphor . . . has a peculiar importance." [16] Furthermore, when one observes how the images and key words could have grown out of one another, it becomes evident that Sonnet 125 has an intricate logic of its own (see p. 136).[17]

Style and Structure

If one defines style broadly as features of selection and arrangement, some of my preceding remarks undoubtedly fall under this heading. The schema for Sonnet 125 suggests the probable (subconscious) verbal structure of the poem, the kind that is necessarily present in all the Sonnets. Other kinds of structure, grammatical, rhetorical, logical, and so on, serve to organize and develop the subject of each Sonnet, and although certain characteristic structures recur, there are almost as many different types of organization as there are particular subjects. Thus everyone who generalizes about *the* structure of the Sonnets, who offers a paradigm of the typical poem, is bound to be in error. T. W. Baldwin, taking the division into three quatrains and a couplet very seriously, regards the Sonnets as rhetorico-logical arguments in distinct parts:

> In the sonnets, the first quatrain is always *propositio*, the couplet is always intended to be some form of *complexio* or *conclusio*. The second quatrain is regularly some form of *ratio*. The third quatrain then has its choice from the numerous possibilities of the other two sections, whether we call them *rationis confirmatio* and *exornatio* with *Ad Herennium*, or *propositionis assumptio* and *assumptionis ratio* with Erasmus, or *confirmatio* and *confutatio* with Brinsley, or still other terms employed by anyone else. This is the literary-logic of Shakespeare's day and this is what he uses in his sonnets.[18]

C. S. Lewis, a far more sensitive and perceptive reader of the Sonnets, says more cautiously that the rhetorical structure is often that of theme and variations, as in *Lucrece*. The variations more often than not precede the theme, and there is usually an application which connects the theme of the particular sonnet with what may be called the 'running' theme of that part of the sequence to which it belongs.[19]

As his fine discussion draws to a close, he generalizes more freely:

They very seldom present or even feign to present passionate thought growing and changing in the heat of a situation; they are not dramatic. The end of each is clearly in view from the beginning, the theme already chosen. Instead of a single developing thought we get what musicians call an 'arrangement,' what we might call a pattern or minuet, of thoughts and images. There are arithmetical elements in the beauty of this pattern as in all formal beauty, and its basic principle is *idem in alio*.[20]

The last phrase might have come from F. W. Bateson, who, although he does not discuss the Sonnets directly, asserts that Elizabethan poetry is characterized by repetitive structure:

The diction of the Elizabethan poets was characterized . . . by the glosses and amplification of "copie." Their words and phrases are reinforced by secondary words and phrases which seem to add little or nothing to the original meaning. . . . In Spenser, therefore, . . . and the other Elizabethan poets the repetitive structure is inextricable from the repetitive diction. The formula . . . is a series of variations upon a single initial idea. . . . Elizabethan diction and Elizabethan structure are two aspects of the same process, the one functioning within the smaller unit of the sentence and the other within the larger unit of the poem.[21]

As one reads the Sonnets he finds that he can agree with some of these statements some of the time, with none of them all of the time. For example, Baldwin's assertion

138

regarding *propositio* is supported by those Sonnets which open with some kind of generalization (53, 54, 57), but it is refuted by others which confirm Lewis' observation that variations often *precede* the theme (12, 64). On the other hand, his term *conclusio,* like Lewis' "application," only serves to conceal variety, since it is vague and broad enough to cover every function of the couplet: summarizing the sense of the poem (88, 89); introducing a qualification, alternative, or contradiction (60, 121); both summarizing and qualifying (53); continuing the sense of the last quatrain (35, 90); and so on.[22] Bateson's comments on repetitive diction are generally irrelevant, however many glosses and amplifications and repeated words the Sonnets may contain; for the expansions, often metaphorical, do "add" something to the meaning of the poem, and the repetitions are usually thematic (93, 152), deliberately clever (43, 135), or emphatic (40), or all three at once. As for Lewis' *idem in alio* principle, crudely approximated by Bateson's "variations upon a single initial idea," one must admit that it is so extremely elastic as to fit quite different Sonnets (73, 94, 125), though in quite different ways, but how does it apply to a poem like Sonnet 41?

Another, more statistical, approach to structure and style is through what Miss Josephine Miles calls "mode," a basic kind of sentence structure. She distinguishes three modes, "clausal," "phrasal," and "balanced," and finds that not only does one type of sentence structure predominate in a poet's work but also that one mode tends to "predominate in the poetry of a generation." [23] The Sonnets exemplify the balanced mode (one adjective and verb per line) of the late sixteenth century (1570–1600):

> What are the simple signs of that classically balanced poetry for which the late Elizabethans then strove? A thoroughly symmetrical proportioning, an inner onomatopoeia and harmony of sound along with the tight outward rhyme,[24] a sensory

and emotional vocabulary. This was the less active, more responsive world of the Shakespearean sonnet, clauses balanced by modifying phrases, and some of the need for connectives smoothed away, in a proportioning of ten adjectives to twenty nouns to ten verbs in ten lines . . . Shakespeare's first sonnet is near the pattern. . . .

After quoting the first Sonnet, she goes on to say,

adjectives and verbs are nearly balanced here, because many clausal constructions have been made phrasal, in the classical fashion. "But then, contracted," and "self-substantial," and "making a famine," and "And tender churl," all by participial, appositional, or compounding construction, turn verbs to adjectives, smooth the transitions, integrate the sound.[25]

The most useful comments here are, as one would expect, the grammatical; for the rest, they only tell us (or hint at) what we already know—that the Sonnets are generally mellifluous, with moderately varied rhythms and frequent alliteration and assonance; that the line is the metrical unit (and often the unit of sense); that the vocabulary is restricted by the range of interests.[26] About the value of the raw statistics one may have deep reservations. Doubtless it is desirable to know something about the distribution of grammatical elements if only for purposes of comparison with other poets; but—and this is hardly fair to Miss Miles in view of her intentions —it might be even more profitable to gather statistics on the characteristics or the elements themselves. Perhaps the number of verbs or adjectives per line is not as important as their kind of function: an investigation of the proportion of transitive to intransitive verbs might bear out Fenollosa's contention that the superiority of Shakespeare's language lies in his persistent use of many transitive verbs.

All that my carping at these various heroic efforts to generalize about the style of the Sonnets amounts to is simply this: no one has ever succeeded in defining their special qualities, chiefly because they are so many and, within certain limits, so varied. One is reduced to uttering the broadest generalities or to discussing the individual poem. The easiest things one can do—counting the comparisons and sentences per quatrain or in the whole Sonnet, noting the distribution of argument in relation to metrical pattern—are probably also the least illuminating, and hence not worth the doing. The more difficult kinds of comparing, classifying, and abstracting may be far more valuable, but the result is usually only a complex intangible, a sense of what distinguishes these Sonnets from all others. To compare Shakespeare with contemporary poets is only to accumulate differences that do not really define his uniqueness. The traditional comparison is with Daniel's sonnets; despite a few superficial resemblances in imagery and diction, Shakespeare's differ radically in rhythm, tone, texture, and vitality of language.[27] On the other side of the fence stand the poems of Donne. Again, though one discovers a subtle complexity of language, a use of associative structure, intensity of emotion, rich texture, and colloquial tone and idiom in both, the striking differences are much more important than the similarities.[28] The Sonnets of Shakespeare are neither Elizabethan nor Metaphysical; in a sense they are both. Our last resort is Eliot's gnomic utterance, "The sonnet of Shakespeare is not merely such and such a pattern, but a precise way of thinking and feeling"; or better still, Coleridge's mature opinion that Shakespeare's language "is entirely his own," that the "construction" of his "sentences, whether in verse or prose, is the necessary and homogeneous vehicle of his peculiar manner of thinking," and that the "body and substance of his works came out of the unfathomable depths of his own oceanic mind." In short, what is concluded that we should conclude anything.

Notes

INTRODUCTION.

[1] Wordsworth's comment was written in the second volume of a copy of Robert Anderson's *Works of the British Poets* (1793). On Nov. 2, 1803, Coleridge refuted it in a note written to his son Hartley in this same volume. He rejects Wordsworth's opinion and sums up his own favorable characterization of the Sonnets in this sentence: "I see no elaborate obscurity and very little quaintness—nor do I know any sonnets that will bear such frequent reperusal: so rich in metre, so full of thought and *exquisitest* diction." *Coleridge's Miscellaneous Criticism*, ed. T. M. Raysor (Cambridge, Mass., 1936), pp. 454–455.

Wordsworth's enumeration of the "heavy" faults of the Sonnets was probably influenced by Anderson's "editorial" comments on them. It is only fair to Wordsworth to add that by 1815 he had become a warm admirer of these poems. See his "Essay, Supplementary to the Preface" (1815), *The Poetical Works of Wordsworth*, ed. T. Hutchinson, rev. E. De Selincourt (Oxford, 1904), p. 745.

[2] Late in life Coleridge, the century's supreme reader of poetry, echoed his note of 1803 when he remarked that the Sonnets were characterized by "boundless fertility and laboured condensation of thought, with perfection of sweetness in rhythm and metre. These are the essentials in the budding of a great poet." *Specimens of the Table Talk of the Late Samuel Taylor Coleridge*, ed. H. N. Coleridge, 2 vols. (London, 1835), II, 181.

[3] This sentence is based on I. A. Richards' *The Philosophy of Rhetoric* (New York, 1936), pp. 38–40. My assumptions about language and poetry are similar to those embodied in this work and in his *Practical Criticism* (London, 1929).

[4] An exception by definition is the corona, a special type of sequence in which the first line of the first sonnet is repeated as the last line of the final sonnet; the last line of the first sonnet is repeated as the first line of the second, and so on. The two well-known English coronas are Chapman's *A Coronet for His Mistress Philosophy* (1595) and Donne's *La Corona* (1607?).

⁵ T. E. Mommsen, "Introduction," *Petrarch: Sonnets and Songs,* trans. A. M. Armi (New York, 1946), p. xxix, hereafter cited as Mommsen.

⁶ See C. S. Lewis' sensible remarks on the character of the sonnet sequence in his *English Literature in the Sixteenth Century* (Oxford, 1954), pp. 327–328, 490–491.

⁷ Notable exceptions in their rejection of the myth of two groups are Sidney Lee, H. E. Rollins (the best modern editor of the Sonnets), and L. C. Knights. See Lee's *A Life of William Shakespeare,* new ed. (London, 1915), pp. 165–166; Rollins' excellent brief introduction to his Crofts Classics edition, *William Shakespeare: Sonnets* (New York, 1951); and Knights's able essay, "Shakespeare's Sonnets," *Explorations* (New York, 1947), p. 56. This essay was first published in *Scrutiny,* III (1934), 133–160.

⁸ E.g., "in the first series, I–CXXVI, a continuous story is conducted through various stages to its termination." Edward Dowden (ed.), *The Sonnets of William Shakespeare* (London, 1881), p. 24. A more recent example of this view is provided by Brooke's assertion that, when some of the poems have been suitably rearranged, "the Sonnets tell a plain and steadfast story." Tucker Brooke (ed.), *Shakespeare's Sonnets* (New York, 1936), p. 28.

⁹ See Mommsen, p. xxxiii, and F. De Sanctis, *A History of Italian Literature,* trans. Joan Redfern, 2 vols. (New York, 1931), I, 275.

CHAPTER 1.

¹ Pooler's comment in the Arden edition of the Sonnets is worth quoting. "The first nineteen Sonnets are indeed closely connected; they advise marriage and promise immortality, and the two subjects are dovetailed together thus: xv. is the first to say that Shakespeare is immortalising his friend in verse; xvi., a continuation of xv., reverts to the subject of marriage; xvii. includes both subjects; xviii. and xix. only immortalisation by verse." *The Works of Shakespeare: Sonnets,* ed. C. K. Pooler, 3rd ed. (London, 1943), p. xxviii.

² The text followed throughout is that of the Crofts Classics edition: *William Shakespeare: Sonnets,* ed. H. E. Rollins (New York, 1951).

³ Cf. Sidney's *Astrophel and Stella,* ed. A. Pollard (London, 1888), No. 18 (ll. 1–8):
> With what sharpe checkes I in my self am shent
> When into Reason's audite I do go,
> And by just counts my self a banckrout know
> Of all those goods which heav'n to me hath lent;
> Unable quite to pay even Nature's rent,
> Whiche unto it by birthright I do ow;
> And, which is worse, no good excuse can show,
> But that my wealth I have most idly spent!

⁴ The text for quotations from the plays and from poems other than the Sonnets is *The Complete Works of William Shakespeare,* ed. W. J. Craig (London, 1904).

⁵ "*Given* thee to *give*" (l. 6) is an example of *traductio* or *polyptoton*

(the repetition of a word stem), one of Shakespeare's favorite figures of rhetoric.

⁶ The ancient and natural connection between offspring and usury is suggested by the Greek word *tokos*, which has the senses offspring, child, son, and interest on a loan (cf. the word "increase"). There is a play on both meanings in Plato's *Republic* 507, and Shakespeare's phrase "a breed for barren metal" (*Merch.* I.iii.135) combines both.

⁷ Adams, *A Life of William Shakespeare* (Boston, 1923), p. 177.

⁸ See *A New Variorum Edition of Shakespeare: The Sonnets*, ed. H. E. Rollins, 2 vols. (Philadelphia, 1944), I, 16; hereafter cited as *Variorum*.

⁹ "Mr. Empson's Muddles," *Southern Review*, IV (1938), 330, hereafter cited as Ransom. In this review-article Ransom discusses William Empson's *English Pastoral Poetry* (New York, 1938), the American reprint of *Some Versions of Pastoral* (London, 1935), which contains an intelligent but rather uneven chapter on Sonnet 94, "They That Have Power."

¹⁰ Ransom, pp. 330–331. The last sentence refers to Sonnets 40–42, especially Sonnet 41.

¹¹ Dowden, ed., *The Sonnets of William Shakespere* (London, 1881), pp. 258–259.

¹² Wordsworth (*The Poetical Works of Wordsworth*, ed. T. Hutchinson, rev. E. De Selincourt [Oxford, 1904], p. 745, n. 2), in his "Essay, Supplementary to the Preface" (1815), called attention to twenty-seven Sonnets as exhibiting "various merits of thought and language," among them Sonnets 91, 92, 97, and 98; Sonnet 94 is conspicuous by its absence.

¹³ "False face must hide what the false heart doth know" (*Macb.* I.vii.82).

¹⁴ Dowden, p. 2.

¹⁵ There are no solid clues to the sex of the friend addressed in Sonnets 87–93. If one recalls that Shakespeare refers to the handsome youth addressed in Sonnets 40–42 as "my love" (40, ll. 1, 3), the vocative "love" in Sonnet 89 (l. 5) may suggest a man; but in Sonnets 149 (l. 13) and 151 (l. 14) he calls a woman "love." However, certain details of Sonnets 95 and 96 which seem consonant with the greater degree of social freedom enjoyed by men may suggest that the poet may well be addressing a young man here and hence in the whole group. Note, for example, the hints of repeated and flagrant sexual sport, the social implications of "gentle" (96, l. 2), and the seduction reference in "lead away" (96, l. 11). Furthermore, Sonnet 95 ends in a phallic proverb; cf. "edge" in *Ham.* III.ii.263–264.

¹⁶ One can make a good case for Sonnet 87 as the last of the Rival Poet group (Sonnets 78–87) as well as the first of this one, and hence as a kind of bridge between them.

¹⁷ I borrow these definitions from I. A. Richards' fine discussion of love in *How to Read a Page* (New York, 1942), pp. 153–156. (Needless to say, *agapé* is not simply Christian love any more than *eros* is merely sexual.) See also A. E. Taylor's lucid remarks on love in *Plato: The Man and His Work* (Meridian, 1956), p. 223.

¹⁸ Euripides, *Orestes*, 667, quoted in the Aristotelian *Magna Moralia*,

1212[b], trans. St. George Stock, in *The Works of Aristotle*, ed. W. D. Ross (Oxford, 1915), vol. IX. (The same line is quoted in Aristotle's *Nicomachean Ethics*, 1169[b].) The point is made in the *Nicomachean Ethics* (1169[b]), *Eudemian Ethics* (1245[b]), and *Magna Moralia* (1213[a]), each of which contains a lengthy discussion of friendship, that even the self-sufficient or happy man needs friends. For other passages that seem relevant to Sonnet 94, see *Magna Moralia*, 1184[b] and 1210[b].

[19] Plato discusses the corruption of the best or philosophic natures in *The Republic* (trans. F. M. Cornford [London, 1941]); two passages from his discussion seem relevant to this Sonnet: ". . . all the good things of life, as they are called, corrupt and distract the soul: beauty, wealth, strength, powerful connections, and so forth" (491), and ". . . given the right instruction, it [the best nature] must grow to the full flower of excellence; but if the plant is sown and reared in the wrong soil, it will develop every contrary defect, unless saved by some miracle" (492).

Compare Johnson's remark in *The Rambler*, No. 38: "Even the gifts of nature, which may truly be considered as the most solid and durable of all terrestrial advantages, are found, when they exceed the middle point, to draw the possessor into many calamities easily avoided by others that have been less bountifully enriched or adorned."

[20] For the proverb, see *Variorum*, I, 234. The first to cite Angelo was Thomas Tyler in his edition of *Shakespeare's Sonnets* (London, 1890), p. 253.

[21] I. A. Richards, *Principles of Literary Criticism* (New York, 1945), p. 250.

[22] Morris Tilley quotes the Latin saying under the proverb H170, "To be able to do Harm and not to do it is noble," in *A Dictionary of the Proverbs in England in the Sixteenth and Seventeenth Centuries* (Ann Arbor, Mich., 1950). Under this proverb he also cites Sonnet 94 and Sidney's *Arcadia*, Bk. II, xv.I.246: "But the more power he hath to hurt, the more admirable is his praise, that he will no hurt."

[23] *The Manual of Epictetus* in *The Stoic and Epicurean Philosophers*, ed. W. J. Oates (New York, 1940), p. 468. Cf. also the *Fragments*, p. 459, and the opening chapter of the *Discourses*, pp. 224–226. English versions of the *Manual* were published in 1567 (trans. James Sanford) and 1610 (trans. John Healey).

[24] *Variorum*, I, 234.

[25] The question of whether there are principles underlying Shakespeare's punctuation has been debated for some years. Percy Simpson (*Shakespearian Punctuation*, Oxford, 1911), A. W. Pollard, J. Dover Wilson, and G. B. Harrison represent those scholars who believe that the punctuation of many Shakespearean texts is rhetorical or dramatic rather than syntactical or grammatical. This general view has been opposed, often rather vehemently, by such distinguished scholars as G. L. Kittredge and S. A. Tannenbaum. For example, in *The Handwriting of the Renaissance* (New York, 1930), Tannenbaum asserts that "in the matter of punctuation marks, . . . writers and printers of the Renaissance period were, if possible, even more lawless and haphazard than as regards spelling and capitalization" (p. 139), and

146

he later lists ten points against the "extravagant and fantastic" claim of the Simpson school (pp. 148–152). However, to judge from Peter Alexander's British Academy lecture of 1945, "Shakespeare's Punctuation," this school (in modified form) is now in the ascendant. Alexander offers two useful punctuation rules "devised by the late Mr. Alfred E. Thiselton." The first is, "Where a clause, phrase, or even a word is interposed in the direct line of construction, a comma is often not found at the beginning of the interposition, but the resumption of the direct line of construction is marked by a comma at its close" (p. 18); the second, "Where there is more than one interposition in the direct line of construction, or where an interposition involves intervening punctuation, there is a tendency to mark the resumption of that line by a semi-colon or a colon. Sometimes even an interposition without intervening punctuation is sufficient to support a semi-colon or a colon" (p. 19). Although the second rule seems to apply to the colon which appears at the end of the quatrain in the Quarto text of Sonnet 94, as far as I can see neither rule sheds any light on the comma within l. 2.

Since the punctuation of the Quarto is either inconsistent or not always intelligible, one must decide each case on its own merits. However, I believe we are becoming more and more reluctant to agree with Johnson and other early editors of Shakespeare that the punctuation is wholly in the editor's power. A recent careful study of the Quarto provides some evidence for a system of sorts. See Albert H. Carter, "The Punctuation of Shakespeare's *Sonnets* of 1609," *Joseph Quincy Adams Memorial Studies*, eds. J. G. McManaway *et al.* (Washington, D.C., 1948), pp. 409–428. See also Charles C. Fries, "Shakespearian Punctuation," in *Studies in Shakespeare, Milton, and Donne* (New York, 1925), pp. 67–86; Walter J. Ong, "Historical Backgrounds of Elizabethan and Jacobean Punctuation Theory," *PMLA*, LIX (1944), 349–360; Laura Riding and Robert Graves, *A Survey of Modernist Poetry* (New York, 1928), pp. 62–81. On the merits and demerits of the text of 1609, see *Variorum*, II, 1–18.

[26] A Schmidt, *Shakespeare-Lexicon*, 2 vols. (Berlin, 1886), s.v. "slow."

[27] See the epigraph to the chapter. Rogers is quoted in Lily Campbell's *Shakespeare's Tragic Heroes* (New York, 1960), p. 96.

[28] "Graces" (favors, benefits, gifts) may suggest those superficial personal qualities that constitute charm (v. Sonnet 96), but glosses on the Parable of the Talents in the Geneva Bible (rev. ed., 1584) and many Renaissance works equate the graces with gifts of God. I take "nature's riches" to refer to rich gifts of Nature, and in medieval tradition the gifts of Nature (as opposed to those of Fortune) are generally considered to be one's endowments of body and soul or mind. On the gifts or goods of Nature, Fortune, and Grace, see Chaucer's *Parson's Tale*, ll. 450 ff., in *The Works of Geoffrey Chaucer*, ed. F. N. Robinson, 2nd ed. (Cambridge, Mass., 1957). Cf. also *The Merchant's Tale*, ll. 1311 ff., and *The Physician's Tale*, ll. 19–29, 293 ff. The general classification of various goods goes back at least as far as Plato (*Euthyd.*, 279A–B; *Phil.*, 48E; *Laws*, 743E) and Aristotle (*Nic. Eth.*, 1098^b).

[29] Cf. Donne's "Good Morrow," ed. H. Grierson (London, 1933), l. 16: "true plain hearts doe in the faces rest"; and *Ham.* IV.vii.109–110: "are you like the painting of a sorrow, / A face without a heart?"

[30] Of course by the law of the excluded middle "their" should refer to *either* lords *or* stewards, but poetry is not logic and Shakespeare may well have had both references in mind. Since it has been taken both ways and one is as likely as the other, I see no reason to choose between them.

[31] For an extreme case of stewardship as slavery, see Sonnets 57 and 58.

[32] On her deathbed Elizabeth was told that "though she had been long a great Queen here upon earth, yet shortly she was to yield an accompt of her stewardship to the King of Kings." *Life in Shakespeare's England,* ed. J. Dover Wilson (Pelican, 1944), p. 260. It was a commonplace of medieval political theory that the ruler is God's steward. See, for example, *R. II.* III.iii.77–78, IV.i.125–126. Cf. Calvin's *Institutes* (trans. Allen), III.vii.5: ". . . whatever God has conferred on us, which enables us to assist our neighbour, we are the stewards of it, and must one day render an account of our stewardship."

[33] Geneva gloss (rev. ed., 1584) on the Parable of the Talents (Luke 19: 22).

[34] Cf. Sonnet 54, ll. 9–12, and note the use of "sweet" in ll. 1–4 of the same sonnet.

[35] *The Whole Works of . . . Taylor,* ed. R. Heber, 15 vols. (London, 1839), XI, 314.

[36] Cf. *A.Y.L.* II.iii.10–13:

Know you not, master, to some kind of men
Their graces serve them but as enemies?
No more do yours: your virtues, gentle master,
Are sanctified and holy traitors to you.

[37] Shakespeare's moral reprobation is frequently manifested by comparisons which have disease and foul odors as their vehicles.

[38] Cf. *John* III.i.51–54:

At thy birth, dear boy,
Nature and Fortune join'd to make thee great:
Of Nature's gifts thou mayst with lilies boast
And with the half-blown rose.

Incidentally, no matter what kind of lily Shakespeare has in mind—and he is probably thinking of the Madonna lily—it would be regarded as having medicinal value.

[39] Cf. *The Raigne of King Edward the Third,* II.i.434–453, in *The Shakespeare Apocrypha,* ed. Tucker Brooke (Oxford, 1908):

The greater man, the greater is the thing,
Be it good or bad, that he shall vndertake:
An vnreputed mote, flying in the Sunne,
Presents a greater substaunce then it is:
The freshest summers day doth soonest taint
The lothed carrion that it seemes to kisse:
Deepe are the blowes made with a mightie Axe:
That sinne doth ten times agreuate it selfe,

That is committed in a holie place:
An euill deed, done by authoritie,
Is sin and subbornation: Decke an Ape
In tissue, and the beautie of the robe
Adds but the greater scorne vnto the beast.
A spatious field of reasons could I vrge
Betweene his glorie, daughter, and thy shame:
That poyson shewes worst in a golden cup;
Darke night seemes darker by the lightning flash;
Lillies that fester smel far worse then weeds;
And euery glory that inclynes to sin,
The shame is treble by the opposite.

The passage restates the point of the Sonnet's sestet. Despite the "Lillies that fester" line, it is of no value in dating the poem, since it is impossible to say which was written first.

⁴⁰ There is nothing in recent criticism of the Sonnets which would affect my views on Sonnet 94. The poem is not discussed in J. B. Leishman's very interesting *Themes and Variations in Shakespeare's Sonnets* (London, 1961), and there is little or no interpretation in Claes Schaar's useful work, *An Elizabethan Sonnet Problem: Shakespeare's Sonnets, Daniel's Delia, and Their Literary Background* (Lund, 1960). Albert S. Gérard's "The Stone as Lily: A Discussion of Shakespeare's Sonnet XCIV," *Shakespeare Jahrbuch*, 96 (1960), 155–160, is a resolute attempt to read the ironies and ambiguity out of the poem. Gérard misreads the octave and oversimplifies the whole sonnet.

CHAPTER 2.

¹ William Empson, *Seven Types of Ambiguity* (London, 1930; 2nd ed., rev., 1947). See also Arthur H. King, "Some Notes on Ambiguity in *Henry IV* Part I," *Studia Neophilologica*, XIV (1941–1942), 161–183.

² H. C. Beeching, ed., *The Sonnets of Shakespeare* (Boston, 1904), p. 100, hereafter cited as Beeching.

³ R. M. Alden, ed., *The Sonnets of Shakespeare* (Boston, 1916), p. 175.

⁴ George Wyndham, ed., *The Poems of Shakespeare* (London, 1898), pp. cxii and 300, hereafter cited as Wyndham.

⁵ Dowden, ed., *The Sonnets of William Shakespere* (London, 1881), pp. 243–244. Cf. p. 31 of his introduction. Hereafter cited as Dowden.

⁶ Baldensperger separates Sonnets 69 and 70, though he keeps them in the same group. See *Les Sonnets de Shakespeare* (Berkeley, 1943). For the arrangements of Bray and Walsh, see *Variorum*, II, 113 ff.

⁷ Beeching, p. lxiv. One need not be committed to any views on the order of the Quarto to see that 69 and 70 are connected. Sense, general subject, pronouns, key words, and rimes all indicate that they belong together.

⁸ *Ibid.*, p. 100. Note also that on p. lxiv he quotes ll. 9–10 of 69

and says it is implied that the friend's deeds "were not good deeds."

⁹ J. W. Lever, *The Elizabethan Love Sonnet* (London, 1956), p. 214, hereafter cited as Lever.

¹⁰ *Ibid.* The first half of the second sentence refers to Sonnet 67 (ll. 1–4). In regard to the rank smell of weeds as "Shakespeare's favorite image . . . ," see n. 17 below.

¹¹ See *ibid.*, pp. 172–173, for his general approach to the Sonnets.

¹² *Ibid.*, p. 193. The iterative image of the rose is certainly not used at random, but I can't see in what sense it is structural despite Lever's claims for it here.

¹³ *Ibid.*, pp. 214–215. In a valuable edition of all the poems, a more recent commentator falls back on the frank admission of inconsistency: "The sonnet [70] as it stands is inconsistent with the sonnet which precedes it, but we should remember that the precise order in which sonnets were written has never been established and the poem may have been written before Shakespeare was aware of anything in the young friend deserving reproof. We should also remember that a series of poems written over a number of years is not likely to be free of inconsistency." Edward Hubler, ed., *Shakespeare's Songs and Poems* (New York, 1959), p. 76, hereafter cited as Hubler, ed.

¹⁴ The sex of the friend addressed in Sonnets 69 and 70 is not certain, though the tone and sense of 70 may suggest a young man. Masculine pronouns are frequent in the linked Sonnets 67 and 68, and 66–70 may form a loose group. Furthermore, the last line of 69 may be taken as a reference to the situation set forth in ll. 1–4 of 67, but I think these lines refer primarily to the evil *world* of Sonnet 66. Thus, though the friend may well be a young man, one can't be sure, and if I use "he" on occasion it is chiefly as a convenience.

¹⁵ Nearly every modern text of this Sonnet contains three emendations of the Quarto (1609) text: *due* for Q *end* (l. 3), *Thy* for Q *Their* (l. 5), and *soyle* (*soil*) for Q *solye* (l. 14). According to most editors the common Q error of *their* for *thy* occurs fifteen times, but in at least two or three instances—this is not one of them—*their* may well be the correct reading.

¹⁶ The latter reading is that of T. G. Tucker, ed., *The Sonnets of Shakespeare* (Cambridge, 1924), p. 145, hereafter cited as Tucker.

¹⁷ "Rank" conveys moral disgust in Sonnet 121 (l. 12), *Meas.* (III.i.98), *W.T.* (I.ii.76), *Oth.* (III.iii.232), *Ham.* (III.ii.268; iii.36; iv.92, 148, 152); more than half of these contexts are sexual, and "weeds" occurs in two of them (*Hamlet*), as well as in two other sexual contexts, *Oth.* (IV.ii.68), cited by Lever, and *Temp.* (IV.i.21). Cf. Donne's Elegie IV: *The Perfume* (l. 24), "The sinnes of her owne youths ranke lustinesse," and Satyre I (l. 38), "ranke itchie lust, desire, and love."

¹⁸ The possibility that "solye" is a spelling of "sully" seems rather slight.

¹⁹ Tucker, pp. 145–146.

²⁰ See, for example, pp. 48–49 and n. 47 below.

²¹ Quoted in C. K. Pooler, *The Works of Shakespeare: Sonnets*, 3rd ed. (London, 1943), p. 71.

[22] Sonnet 67 provides cold comfort for those taking this position if one stresses its connection with 66; that is, in the light of Sonnet 66, the first quatrain of 67 has a general sense which it does not have when viewed in isolation.

[23] "Soil" as moral blemish is frequently used in sexual contexts. See *Meas.* (V.141), *Much* (III.ii.5), *Ham.* (I.iii.15), *Troi.* (II.ii.148), and *Antony* (I.iv.24). Lines 7–10 (or at least 9–10) of Sonnet 70 also tend to support my view that the charge concerns sins of the flesh.

[24] He displays a remarkable capacity for observing the old Greek proverb, "Know your friend's habits, do not hate them" and Cassius' advice in *Caesar* (IV.iii.85), "A friend should bear his friend's infirmities."

[25] There are two common emendations of the Q text here: *art* for Q *are* (l. 1) and *Thy* for Q *Their* (l. 6). The first seems unnecessary.

[26] With lines 2, 7, and 9 of Sonnet 70 cf. *Ham.* I.iii.38 ff.:
> Virtue herself 'scapes not calumnious strokes;
> The canker galls the infants of the spring
> Too oft before their buttons be disclos'd,
> And in the morn and liquid dew of youth
> Contagious blastments are most imminent.

[27] Lever, however, makes no effort to support his assertion. *Measure for Measure* is in some respects a large-scale example of Shakespearean casuistry. See Wylie Sypher, "Shakespeare as Casuist," *Sewanee Review*, LVIII (1950), 262–280.

[28] See E. A. Abbott, *A Shakespearian Grammar*, 3rd ed. (London, 1870), sec. 315.

[29] Cf. the case of "common" in Sonnet 69.

[30] *All's W.* II.i.184–185; *R.III* I.ii.246–249; V.iii.119 ("prime of youth"); *3 H.VI* II.i.21–24 ("prime of youth").

[31] *T.G.V.* I.i.42–50. In his edition Hubler (p. 76) glosses "prime" and "young days" as "youth" without further comment.

[32] *L.L.L.* I.ii.15; *Ham.* II.ii. 11–12.

[33] See Sonnets 30, 53 (discussed below), 57, 73, 74, 75, 129, and so on.

[34] Doubtless I can be charged with simply reversing traditional procedure and reading Sonnet 70 in terms of 69. I can only reply that I feel obliged to take 69 seriously because, apart from the somewhat diplomatic use of "common," it is direct and unequivocal in its charge. But even those who weigh 70 most heavily (as the great qualification to 69) cannot deny that it does have rather uneasy qualifications, that it does give the impression of being a lame and forced excuse.

[35] The usual emendation of *thy* for Q *their* occurs in l. 11.

[36] "Thy inward love of heart" is a hard phrase which may be taken as equivalent to love of thy inward heart or perhaps inward love of thy heart. In any case "inward" has the obvious sense internal and may also signify fervent, intense, and earnest.

[37] Dowden, p. 234; italics mine. Like all the other commentators, Dowden gives Sonnets 53 and 54 a routine reading even though he puts them in this absence group.

[38] Cf. Sonnet 52 and also Sonnets 75 and 118.

[39] Cf. the similar Sonnet 61.

[40] "Separable spite" is equivalent to spiteful separation.

[41] Since Sonnet 54, which continues and expands the couplet of 53, is addressed to a beauteous and lovely youth, it follows that Sonnet 53 is also. This is the only reference to the sex of the person addressed in the whole group (Sonnets 43–58). Sonnets 40–42 are addressed to a handsome youth, and there are male references in Sonnet 63.

[42] Lines 5–8 and 12–13 of Sonnet 53 may be used to gloss the pregnant seventh line of Sonnet 20. Cf. also ll. 1–8 of Sonnet 106.

[43] Coleridge, *Aids to Reflection* (Burlington, Vt., 1840), p. 71, n.

[44] See A. E. Taylor, *Plato: The Man and His Work* (New York, 1956), p. 230, hereafter cited as Taylor.

[45] Wyndham, p. 287. He cites good examples from Hoby and Spenser. A short historical outline of Renaissance Platonism is given by P. O. Kristeller in *The Classics and Renaissance Thought* (Cambridge, Mass., 1955), pp. 48–69. "Shadow" and "substance" are also technical terms of medieval philosophy. See the glossary to *Selections from Medieval Philosophers*, ed. R. McKeon, 2 vols. (New York, 1929–1930), under *substantia, umbra, imago,* and *vestigium.*

[46] It is a Platonic commonplace that "all sensible beauty is itself the expression and shadow of an inward beauty of character" (Taylor, p. 280), and constancy is a kind of inward beauty, as Sonnet 54 emphasizes. See *The Republic,* 402–403, from which the epigraph is taken.

[47] These words are equivalent to "bounteous" or "generous"; for sexual senses see *Oth.* (II.i.165; III.iv.38, 44, 46), *Ham.* (IV.vii.171), *1 H.VI* (V.iv.82). Cf. "liberty" in Sonnet 41.

[48] *Variorum,* I, 143, referring to many commentators.

[49] Leishman, *Themes and Variations in Shakespeare's Sonnets* (London, 1961), pp. 169–170. The line quoted is from *Sonnets pour Hélène,* II.18.

[50] Lever finds these words "charged with sexual suggestion" (p. 213). To the best of my knowledge, he is the only commentator to smell a fault in connection with Sonnet 54, but he does so purely on the basis of its imagery, for he removes it from the context of the absence group. His last paragraph on the poem (p. 213) is crude and careless, even though it is undertaken with the laudable purpose of pointing out that the poet's use of imagery "rather suggests an unresolved conflict in his attitude to the Friend." I tend to agree with this remark, but reading the poem in the light of almost irrelevant contexts like Sonnet 68 is hardly the way to support it. Once again Lever is the victim of his concern with iterative imagery and his eye for superficial resemblances.

[51] Cf. the couplet of Sonnet 93.

[52] The importance of truth as troth (constancy, loyalty, fidelity) is suggested by the many Sonnets using "true" or "truth" in this major sense: 14, 21, 37, 40, 41, 48, 54, 57, 61, 66, 72, 93, 101, 105, 107, 108, 110, 113, 116, 123, 125, 137, 138, 152, and 154. (There are others, of course, like Sonnet 124, which deal with constancy without using either of these words.) See also "The Phoenix and the Turtle."

[53] It is a homily, though a gentle and persuasive one, by virtue of its tone and emblematic method; cf. the sestet of Sonnet 94.

[54] Aristotle, *Rhetoric,* 1367^b–1368^a, trans. J. H. Freese (Cambridge, Mass., 1926).

[55] Cf. Erasmus, *Praise of Folly*, trans. L. F. Dean (Chicago, 1946), p. 84: "Disguised as praise, it [flattery] warns and instructs princes without offense."

[56] C. S. Lewis, *English Literature in the Sixteenth Century* (Oxford, 1954), p. 352.

[57] Even the "realist" Donne can write a poem called "The Undertaking" or "Platonic Love" with these lines:

> But he who lovelinesse within
> Hath found, all outward loathes,
> For he who colour loves, and skinne,
> Loves but their oldest clothes.

[58] See, e.g., Sonnets 41 and 93, "Phoenix" (ll. 65–67), *A.Y.L.* (I.ii.41–43; III.iii.32–33), *Ham.* (III.i.107–109, 111 ff.), and *Troi.* (III.ii. 165–170; V.ii.65, 134–157). Cf. "Beautie and chastitie one place refraine" in *England's Helicon*, ed. H. E. Rollins, 2 vols. (Cambridge, Mass., 1935), I, 223, and II, 157.

Chapter 3.

[1] It is emphatic according to Schmidt, *Shakespeare-Lexicon*, 2 vols. (Berlin, 1886), s.v. "out."

[2] The couplet of Sonnet 33 seems to offer a double excuse: the friend's behavior is as natural and understandable as the obscuring of the sun; even the sun has imperfections, and thus we must expect them in sons of this world (cf. Sonnet 35, ll. 1–5).

[3] Cf. Adams, *A New Variorum Edition of Shakespeare: The Sonnets*, ed. H. E. Rollins, 2 vols. (Philadelphia, 1944), I, 95–96. Of course the senses of these words are adjusted to the general comparison; e.g., "disgrace" signifies disfigurement in reference to the sun, but its common denotation of personal shame and dishonor lies just below the surface.

[4] Cf. Sonnet 109 (l. 11) and *L.L.L.* II.i.47–48.

[5] It also has the face-disgrace rhyme of Sonnet 33 (ll. 6, 8) in its sixth and eighth lines.

[6] A universal emendation in l. 12 is *cross* for Q *losse*.

[7] "Brav'ry," denoting splendor, glory, finery, refers to the sun and the friend's clothes and qualities. "Rotten smoke" is an unhealthy vapor or mist, and "rotten" also means corrupt.

[8] "Disgrace" signifies scar; dishonor.

[9] For the common Shakespearean comparison of tears to pearls, see *Venus*, ll. 979–80; *Lucr.*, ll. 1213, 1553; *T.G.V.* III.i.225; *R. III* IV.iv.322–323; *Lear* IV.iii.23–24.

[10] With ll. 1–5, cf. *Lucr.*, ll. 848–854. Tilley, *A Dictionary of the Proverbs* . . . (Ann Arbor, Mich., 1950), connects three of these lines with the following proverbs: R182, "No Rose without a thorn (prickle)"; C56, "The Canker soonest eats the fairest rose"; M116, "Every Man has (No man is without) his faults."

[11] The sense and diction of Sonnet 120 make it clear that it refers to Sonnets 34 and 35:

> That you were once unkind befriends me now,

153

And for that sorrow which I then did feel
Needs must I under my transgression bow,
4 Unless my nerves were brass or hammered steel.
For if you were by my unkindness shaken,
As I by yours, you've passed a hell of time,
And I, a tyrant, have no leisure taken
8 To weigh how once I suffered in your crime.
O that our night of woe might have rememb'red
My deepest sense how hard true sorrow hits,
And soon to you, as you to me then, tend'red
12 The humble salve which wounded bosoms fits!
But that your trespass now becomes a fee;
Mine ransoms yours, and yours must ransom me.

Only in these Sonnets do the following words appear: "salve" (34, 120), "salving" (35), "ransom" (34, 120), and "needs must" (35, 120); the figure of salving a wound occurs only in these poems, with the example in Sonnet 120 paralleling that in Sonnet 34.

[12] See *Variorum*, I, 77; II, 7 f., 96, 99.

[13] *Ibid.*, I, 101.

[14] Case, quoted in *ibid.*

[15] *Ibid.*

[16] See E. A. Abbott, *A Shakespearian Grammar*, 3rd ed. (London, 1870), sec. 17. C. J. Sisson regards "more" as equivalent to more numerous, greater. *New Readings in Shakespeare*, 2 vols. (Cambridge, 1956), I, 211.

[17] George Wyndham, ed., *The Poems of Shakespeare* (London, 1898), p. 283.

[18] H. C. Beeching, ed., *The Sonnets of Shakespeare* (Boston, 1904), p. 91, hereafter cited as Beeching.

[19] See, for example, in Richard Bernard's *Thesaurus Biblicus* (London, 1644), "amiss," "fault," and "trepass."

[20] Cf. Sonnet 40, ll. 9–10, and also l. 8 of Sonnet 142.

[21] On the whole, the best brief comment on Sonnet 35, inexplicably ignored by the *Variorum*, is that of L. C. Knights, *Explorations* (New York, 1947), p. 65, hereafter cited as Knights: "The first four lines we may say, both in movement and imagery, are typically Spenserian and straightforward. The fifth line begins by continuing the excuses, 'All men make faults,' but with an abrupt change of rhythm Shakespeare turns the generalization against himself: 'All men make faults, and even I in this,' i.e. in wasting my time finding romantic parallels for your sins, as though intellectual analogies ('sence') were relevant to your sensual fault. The painful complexity of feeling (Shakespeare is at the same time tender towards the sinner and infuriated by his own tenderness) is evident in the seventh line, which means both 'I corrupt myself when I find excuses for you' (or 'when I comfort myself in this way') and 'I'm afraid I myself make you worse by excusing your faults'; and although there is a fresh change of tone towards the end (the twelfth line is virtually a sigh as he gives up hope of resolving the conflict), the equivocal 'needs must' and the sweet-sour opposition show the continued civil war of the emotions."

[22] Beeching says that Sonnets 133–136 and 143–144 "deal with the

154

same subject" as Sonnets 40–42, "an intrigue of the poet's friend with a lady unknown" (p. 93).

²³ Rollins follows the majority in emending Q *this selfe* (l. 7) to *thyself*.

²⁴ Tucker's gloss on l. 3 (p. 117) distorts it to fit his interpretation of l. 4. *The Sonnets of Shakespeare* (Cambridge, 1924), hereafter cited as Tucker.

²⁵ "Then" (l. 5) seems to mean since it is so, in that case, and to signify a sequence of inference.

²⁶ Plato (*Rep.*, 424, *Phaedrus*, 278) and Aristotle (*Nic. Eth.*, 1159ᵇ) quote this proverb.

²⁷ See also Sonnets 36, 39, 62, and 134; *The Essays of Montaigne*, trans. E. J. Trechmann, 2 vols. (New York, n.d.), I, 188–189, 190–191; Sir Thomas Browne, *Religio Medici*, part II, sec. 5; Spenser's *The Faerie Queene*, IV.ii.43 (re three brothers); *England's Helicon* (ed. Rollins), II, 196–197.

Tilley cites Sonnets 39 (l. 2) and 42 (l. 13) under the proverb F696, "A Friend is one's second selfe." This proverb lends support to the Quarto's reading, *this selfe*, in l. 7.

²⁸ "Receivest" might be read as take into sexual partnership, and l. 6 as, I cannot blame you because you make use of my love for both of you to achieve your desire.

²⁹ This reading of the second quatrain is generally similar to that of Dowden, *The Sonnets of William Shakespere* (London, 1881), pp. 226–227, hereafter cited as Dowden. The common emendation "thyself," rejected by Wyndham and Tucker Brooke, is unnecessary, for "this selfe" of the Quarto makes very good sense.

³⁰ "Poverty" plays on property.

³¹ Cf. Byrd's *Psalmes, Songs, and Sonnets*, xi in *English Madrigal Verse 1588–1632*, ed. E. H. Fellowes, 2nd ed. (Oxford, 1929), p. 64:

A feigned friend by proof I find
    To be a greater foe
Than he that with a spiteful mind
    Doth seek my overthrow;
For of the one I can beware,
With craft the other breeds my care.

Such men are like the hidden rocks
    Which in the seas do lie,
Against the which each ship that knocks
    Is drowned suddenly.
No greater fraud, nor more injust,
Than false deceit hid under trust.

³² "Lascivious grace" echoes Ovid's *lascive puer* (*Met.*, I, 456); there is no reason to believe that "lascivious" simply means wanton or sportive, as Tucker (p. 118) would have it. Cf. Sonnets 95 and 96 with l. 13.

³³ Dowden, p. 227; Pooler, ed., *The Works of Shakespeare: Sonnets*, 3rd ed. (London, 1943), p. 45, hereafter cited as Pooler.

³⁴ The common emendation of *she* for Q *he* (l. 8) is quite unnecessary.

155

[35] Regarding ll. 1–2 Tyler says, "it may be supposed that Mr. W. H. takes this 'liberty' while Shakespeare is away." *Shakespeare's Sonnets* (London, 1890), hereafter cited as Tyler. I doubt if l. 2 refers to a physical absence, but it is quite possible to take it as Tyler does (perhaps on the grounds that to be out of sight is to be out of mind).

As far as choosing between the general and particular readings of the octave is concerned, I prefer the general and would only add that the poet may have the friend's amour with his mistress in mind too, but I feel it is somewhere in the background. Obviously that affair could easily follow the *general* pattern of the others. There are, of course, other interpretations which would lie somewhere between the two extremes I sketch.

[36] Edward Hubler, *The Sense of Shakespeare's Sonnets* (Princeton, 1952), p. 83.

[37] *Ibid.*, p. 85. Just before quoting from Sonnet 41 Hubler remarks, "She wooed the young man and won him." Tyler says, "the lady was the suitor" (p. 199), and Beeching agrees: "it was the mistress who courted the friend rather than the friend who courted the mistress" (p. lxiv).

[38] Tucker, p. 119.

[39] Commentators are so often compelled to focus their attention on the word, the phrase, or the line that they are apt to forget that the sentence is the unit of meaning.

[40] "Riot" is more or less equivalent to "liberty" (l. 1), both denoting dissoluteness, amoral or unrestrained conduct (v. *Tim.* IV.i.25–28). In some respects it is a stronger word than "liberty," for even its milder senses (tumult, disturbance; revelry, noisy feasting) are rather unfavorable. Pooler notes that the meaning of "liberty" "varies in Shakespeare from the privilege of dispensing with conventions to license in the worst sense" (p. 45). Its range of meaning permits the poet to both excuse and condemn the friend's wrongs at the same time. With its implications here cf. *Ham.* II.i.22 ff. and 31 ff.:

> such wanton, wild, and usual slips
> As are companions noted and most known
> To youth and liberty.

> breathe his faults so quaintly
> That they may seem the taints of liberty,
> The flash and outbreak of a fiery mind,
> A savageness in unreclaimed blood,
> Of general assault.

[41] I may be overreading, but "loving offenders" seems to have three senses: affectionate offenders, or offenders who love each other; offenders through love; offenders of love—the speaker's love for both.

[42] The sense of both the second and third quatrains is against Empson's opinion that l. 8 may go with either what comes before or what comes after it. *Seven Types of Ambiguity*, 2nd ed. (Norfolk, Conn., 1947), p. 51, hereafter cited as Empson. "Approve" denotes test, try, or experience—sexually.

[43] Knights, p. 58. His first sentence looks back to the Sonnet's first

gement; rule, government. With this line cf. the opening of Sonnet
150: "O, from what pow'r hast thou this pow'rful might / With in-
sufficiency my heart to sway?"

[10] "Controlling" may mean reprove; contradict; restrain; command
or dominate.

[11] *Troi.* IV.iv.103–108.

[12] *Antony* III.xi.42–46. Cf. *Meas.* III.ii.243–247, and *Lear* II.iv.72–
86.

[13] "My love" could apply to either a man or woman, but Sonnet 67,
which seems to refer to 66, has "he," and hence the person addressed
here may well be a man.

[14] A partial analogue to Sonnet 66 is the conclusion of the explanatory myth of Mercury and the country maid in the first sestiad
of *Hero and Leander,* ll. 469–484 (*The Works of Christopher Marlowe,* ed. Tucker Brooke, Oxford, 1910):

> Yet as a punishment they added this,
> That he and Pouertie should alwaies kis.
> And to this day is euerie scholler poore,
> Grosse gold from them runs headlong to the boore.
> Likewise the angrie sisters thus deluded,
> To venge themselues on Hermes, have concluded
> That *Midas* brood shall sit in Honors chaire,
> To which the *Muses* sonnes are only heire:
> And fruitfull wits that in aspiring are,
> Shall discontent run into regions farre;
> And few great lords in vertuous deeds shall ioy,
> But be surpris'd with euery garish toy;
> And still inrich the loftie seruile clowne,
> Who with incroching guile keepes learning downe
> Then muse not *Cupids* sute no better sped,
> Seeing in their loues the Fates were iniured.

[15] The subgroup 109–112 consists of two pairs of Sonnets, 109–110
and 111–112. The general similarity of the couplets of 109 and 112
gives the impression that the cluster begins and ends on much the
same note.

[16] There are many words referring to his "sins," for example, "stain,"
"frailties" (109); "offenses," "blenches" (110); "harmful deeds,"
"infection" (111); "shames" (112); "errors" (117); "sick," "diseased"
(118); and "transgression," "trespass" (120).

[17] Lines 1–5 of Sonnet 111 also touch on his reputation.

[18] Line 14 has the common emendation *methinks are* for Q *me
thinkes y'are.*

[19] See, for example, *Variorum,* I, 304–305.

[20] Beeching, *The Sonnets of Shakespeare* (Boston, 1904), p. 120,
hereafter cited as Beeching. Cf. also Tyler, *Shakespeare's Sonnets*
(London, 1890), p. 280, hereafter cited as Tyler, and Pooler, *The
Works of Shakespeare: Sonnets,* 3rd ed. (London, 1943), p. 115, hereafter cited as Pooler.

[21] G. Wilson Knight, *The Mutual Flame* (London, 1955), p. 49 (v.
also p. 48), hereafter cited as Wilson Knight.

[22] Knights, pp. 76–77.

quatrain, which he has just quoted. In regard to Sonnet 19 ("Devouring Time . . .") I would suggest that, like most critics, Knights tends
to overrate Sonnets dealing with mutability. With his remarks on Sonnet 42 cf. Frank Harris (quoted in Alden, ed., *The Sonnets of Shakespeare* [Boston, 1916], p. 115): "This sonnet, with its affected wordplay and wire-drawn consolation, leaves one gaping: Sh's verbal
affections had got into his very blood. To my mind the whole sonnet
is too extravagant to be sincere. . . . None of it rings true except
the first couplet."

[44] Note especially the feeling in the first four lines of Sonnet 40 and
the last six of 41. After quoting the opening of Sonnet 42, Knights de-
clares, "we may say that if Shakespeare had suffered the experience
indicated by a prose *paraphrase* . . . it would have affected him very
differently from *this*" (p. 58). Of course it would; it would have affected him somewhat the way betrayal affects the speaker in Sonnets
40 and 41. Incidentally, these two poems make nonsense of some of
Lever's sweeping remarks on Sonnets 40–42. Overemphasis of 42
seems responsible for this typical comment: "these sonnets . . . show
a marked relaxation of tone and emotional tension" (p. 226); yet 40
has an opening as violent as any in the collection.

[45] M. M. Mahood, *Shakespeare's Wordplay* (London, 1957), p. 91,
hereafter cited as Mahood. Her general approach to the Sonnets is
neatly stated in one paragraph: "The nature of the wordplay in the
Sonnets varies according to whether Shakespeare is too remote or too
near the experience behind the poem or whether he is at a satisfying
dramatic distance from it. When he is detached, the wordplay is a
consciously used, hard-worked rhetorical device. When his complexity
of feeling upon the occasion of a sonnet is not fully realised by him,
the wordplay often reveals an emotional undercurrent which was perhaps hidden from the poet himself. But in the best sonnets the wordplay is neither involuntary nor wilful; it is a skillfully handled means
whereby Shakespeare makes explicit both his conflict of feelings and
his resolution of the conflict" (pp. 91–92). Much of this is valid and
well said, the last sentence in particular, but individual Sonnets often
elude neat generalizations, especially when they depend on assumptions derived from the plays.

[46] Sonnets 56–58 may well form a small group, as Tyler suggests
(p. 214). I have already touched on the place of these three poems in
a large absence group. On the sex of the person addressed, see chap.
ii, n. 41, above.

[47] Miss Mahood's comments (p. 110) on the quatrains of this Sonnet are valuable: "We might paraphrase: [ll. 3–4] 'I have no strong
claims on my time and attention except yours.' But *spend* can have
a more forceful meaning of 'expend' or even 'waste' and this insinuates
an unexpected note of protest: 'Time is too valuable for me to waste it
in this fashion.' The ecclesiastical senses of *hours* and *services* and the
echo of the doxology in 'world without end' serve to buttress the
counterstress set up by this protest; Shakespeare resents the time he
has squandered upon a false devotion. And once this note of resentment has been struck, its reverberations are heard in the over-strong
protestations of 'Nor dare I chide . . .' and 'Nor dare I question.'"

[48] Empson has a fairly good discussion of some examples of this formula, "The A and B of C," pp. 88–101.

[49] The phrase appears in the First Prayer Book of Edward VI (1549) and in all later editions.

[50] The text for these quotations is that of the Geneva Bible (1600). The relevant stanza of the *Te Deum* is quoted in the metrical version of Sternhold and Hopkins, whose versified Psalms were frequently bound up with Geneva and Bishops' Bibles and with the Prayer Book. The Isaiah passage is part of an exhortation to patience.

"World without end" also occurs in Ephesians 3:21 in the Rheims New Testament (1582) and the Authorized Version.

[51] Lawrence Babb, *The Elizabethan Malady* (East Lansing, 1951), p. 5. See also Aquinas, *Summa Theologica*, Ia.80.1; 82.2, 4; Aristotle, *Nic. Eth.*, 1094ᵃ and 1172ᵇ. The general view that "we desire what is good" (*Gorg.*, 468) and that "no one willingly goes to meet evil or what he thinks to be evil" (*Prot.*, 358) goes back at least as far as Socrates and Plato.

[52] Cf. Mahood (p. 110): "The extent to which Shakespeare does chide and question is shown in the last two lines of the sonnet which appear to say: 'Love is so foolishly faithful in your Will Shakespeare that he cannot think ill of you, whatever you do'; but which also say: 'Love is so utterly foolish that, however wilful and perverse you are, it cannot see the wrongness of your behaviour.' In depicting this blend of adulation and contempt, and in all those sonnets where verbal ambiguity is thus used as a deliberate dramatic device, Shakespeare shows that superb insight into states of strongly mixed feelings which enabled him to bring to life a Coriolanus or an Enobarbus."

[53] Erasmus, *The Praise of Folly*, p. 57.

[54] Plato, *Apol.*, 21 and 23. For a good general discussion of "fool" and its implications, see Empson's *The Structure of Complex Words* (Norfolk, Conn., n.d.), pp. 105–124, from which I received several useful suggestions.

[55] Pooler, p. 60; Empson, p. 54. Empson's brief comments, concentrating on ll. 7 and 11, are vitiated by his taking the Quarto punctuation too seriously. It is hard to make sense of the Quarto's comma after "tame," and though the syntax of l. 11 is somewhat ambiguous, it makes the quatrain unnecessarily tautological to regard "your time" as a subject of "belong."

[56] Cf. "liberty" in Sonnet 41 and see n. 40 above.

[57] "Suffer"—to bear with patience and constancy; to bear or undergo pain or distress; "patience"—suffering or enduring (pain, etc.) with calmness; "bide"—to face, encounter; suffer, endure; tolerate, put up with; "sufferance"—distress, pain, suffering; endurance; permission, toleration, acquiescence. C. T. Onions gives the last sense, permission, as the definition of "sufferance" in his *Shakespeare Glossary*, 2nd ed., rev. (Oxford, 1919). "Tame" has the senses submissive, meek, subdued; servile or spiritless, and "tame to sufferance" may be read at least three ways: subdued to pain; submissive to the point of endurance; servile to the point of acquiescence.

[58] "*Check*, a term in falconry, applied to a hawk when she forsakes her proper game, and follows some other inferior kind that crosses her in her flight" (citing *Twel.* III.i.72; II.v.128). A. Dyce, *Glossary*

to the Works of William Shakespeare, rev. 1902), hereafter cited as Dyce. See also John of Shakespeare's Hawking Language," *Univ.* lish (1938), p. 138, for a general discussion o

[59] Cf. *A.Y.L.* II.vii.47–49 ("I must have li a charter . . ."); *R.II.* II.i.197 ("His char rights"); *R.II.* III.i.54 ("You break no privi Cor. II.iii.188 ("Your liberties and the charter I.i.48 ("The air, a charter'd libertine . . .").

[60] Cf. "The charter of thy worth gives thee l. 3).

[61] Cf. the whole of Sonnet 61 with Sonnets between "watch" (to stay awake, keep a devo (to stay awake; hold a late revel) parallels and "sense" in Sonnet 35, for "watch" probabl carouse at night. See Dyce under "wake" for "watch."

CHAPTER 4.

[1] See, for example, Knights, *Explorations* (N 77–78, hereafter cited as Knights; D. A. Travers speare (London, 1938), pp. 46–48; Mark van (New York, 1939), p. 13. Traversi thinks that ness of the action of Time is the "cause" of the of his Sonnets. Cf. his later views in the revise Approach to Shakespeare (Garden City, 1956),

[2] *A New Variorum Edition of Shakespeare: Th* Rollins, 2 vols. (Philadelphia, 1944), I, 174. Variorum.

[3] Abbott, *A Shakespearian Grammar*, 3rd ed. (113, quotes the opening of Sonnet 66 to illustra of "as" (l. 2) to signify "namely."

[4] One of the frequent senses of "cry" is to be phrases "cry mercy, . . . pardon, . . . grace."

[5] Schmidt, *Shakespeare-Lexicon*, 2 vols. (Berlin take "forsworn" to mean perjured here and in Son signify that faith is denied or repudiated on (or victim of perjury, 'sworn away'" as Tucker, *The* speare (Cambridge, 1924), p. 141, puts it. In the c the forswearing (in both senses) was not really v forced to break a commitment or oath and to tak haps any forswearer could claim he was forced (cf. 41).

[6] *Merch.* II.ix.39–45.

[7] *Collected Poems of Sir Thomas Wyatt*, ed. Ke don, 1949), p. 193, hereafter cited as Muir. Cf. Tim "thou bright defiler / Of Hymen's purest bed" (*Tim*

[8] Cf. "disgrace" in Sonnets 33 and 34, where the and dishonored are also relevant.

[9] One of the specialized meanings of "strength" armed forces, troops, army. "Sway" signifies control

[23] The deliberately shocking opening statement is resolutely anti-Platonic: "set beside this paragon [of injustice] the just man in his simplicity and nobleness, one who, in Aeschylus' words, 'would be, not seem, the best.' There must, indeed, be no such meaning; for if his character were apparent, his reputation would bring him honours and rewards, and then we should not know whether it was for their sake that he was just or for justice's sake alone. He must be stripped of everything but justice, and denied every advantage the other enjoyed. Doing no wrong, he must have the worst reputation for wrong-doing, to test whether his virtue is proof against all that comes of having a bad name; and under this lifelong imputation of wickedness, let him hold on his course of justice unwavering to the point of death. And so, when the two men have carried their justice and injustice to the last extreme, we may judge which is the happier." *Rep.*, 361 (trans. F. M. Cornford).

[24] Dowden, *The Sonnets of William Shakespere* (London, 1881), pp. 281–282, hereafter cited as Dowden.

[25] Wilson Knight, p. 51. This is more careful and elaborate than Beeching's brief, ambiguous gloss.

[26] Tyler combines the second and third interpretations in that he regards "which is so deemed" as looking back to ll. 1–2.

[27] Pooler, p. 116. He then sets forth his own qualms about his own reading as well as those of Tyler, Dowden, and Beeching.

[28] Even though I can find only one other possible example of such a use of "just" ("just belief" may be the equivalent of "belief in justice" in *Pericles*), the grammatical usage is frequent in Shakespeare, and, as far as the individual word is concerned, one must always allow for the unique case.

[29] A few passages in Aristotle and Cicero connect honor or reputation with worth, for example, *Rhetoric* 1361ª ("Honour is a token of a reputation for doing good; and those who have already done good are justly and above all honoured . . ."), and especially 1365ª ("honour is a sort of measure of worth") and *De Officiis*, I.xxviii.99 ("indifference to public opinion implies not merely self-sufficiency, but even total lack of principle"). Sir Thomas Elyot has a few sentences on this subject: ". . . we knowe nothinge but by outwarde significations. Honour, wherto reuerence pertayneth, is (as I have said) the rewarde of vertue, whiche honour is but the estimation of people, which estimacion is nat euery where perceyued, but by some exterior signe, and that is either by laudable reporte, or excellencie in vesture, or other thinge semblable"; *The Boke Named The Governour*, III.ii, Everyman's Library ed. (London, n.d.), p. 200. See Curtis Watson, *Shakespeare and the Renaissance Concept of Honor* (Princeton, 1960), for a useful discussion of the whole subject.

[30] Dowden's and Wilson Knight's interpretations of ll. 3–4 may be influenced by ll. 7–8; at any rate both—Knight's to a lesser extent—do anticipate the sense of l. 8 in particular.

[31] Cf. ll. 9–10 of Sonnet 109.

[32] Alden, *The Sonnets of Shakespeare* (Boston, 1916), p. 284, and Brooke, *Shakespeare's Sonnets* (New York, 1936), p. 323, intelligently comment on this line; Wilson Knight renders it as " 'enjoy prying into

and recognizing the secrets of my sexual life'" (p. 50). Most editors accept the definition of "Give salutation to" (affect, stir, tempt) offered by Schmidt and Onions even though it does not fit the context. Note that "salute" in *Troilus* occurs in a lengthy discussion of worth and reputation.

[33] Cf. the end of Donne's *Metempsychosis*: "Ther's nothing simply good, nor ill alone, / Of every quality Comparison / The only measure is, and judge, Opinion."

[34] *Oth.* I.i.61–65. Cf. *Twel.* III.i.155.

[35] Muir, pp. 154–155. For some reason commentators have not cited Wyatt's poem.

[36] Pooler's definition comes from the *N.E.D.*, which gives examples from Wyclif and Lander (1556). Two other *N.E.D.* definitions deserving consideration are "to flourish," with fifteenth-century examples, and "to flourish *in* some respect" (obsolete and rare), with one example from 1546.

[37] Sir Walter Ralegh, *The History of the World* (London, 1687), I.ii.5. (It is obvious that "*in* the Universal" is an error for *of*.) Cf. Gen. 1:26 and Psalms 8:4–8.

[38] *The Discourses* (trans. C. E. Detmold), I.iii.

[39] Babb, *The Elizabethan Malady* (East Lansing, Mich., 1951), pp. 129–130, hereafter cited as Babb.

[40] According to C. S. Lewis, *English Literature in the Sixteenth Century* (Oxford, 1954), p. 507, in Sonnet 129 "progression almost ends with line 5. . . . The next seven lines are largely, though not entirely, variations on the fifth."

[41] Cf. Ralegh's "Conceipt Begotten by the Eyes," especially the fourth and fifth stanzas:

> Desire himselfe runnes out of breath,
> And getting, doth but gaine his death:
> Desire, nor reason hath, nor rest,
> And blinde doth sildome chuse the best,
> Desire attain'd is not desire,
> But as the sinders of the fire . . .

> So fond Desire when it attaines,
> The life expires, the woe remaines.

The text is that of *The Poems of Sir Walter Ralegh*, ed. Agnes M. C. Latham (London, 1951).

[42] Babb, pp. 8, 146.

[43] *Metempsychosis*, ll. 208–210. Cf. "Farewell to Love," ll. 24–25.

[44] *The Anatomy of Melancholy*, ed. A. R. Shilleto, 3 vols. (London, 1893), III, 177.

[45] *Ibid.*, p. 139.

[46] Riding and Graves, *A Survey of Modernist Poetry* (New York, 1928), p. 68.

[47] For example, consider these remarks, *ibid.*, p. 67: "Particularly serious is the interpolation of a comma after *no sooner had;* for this confines the phrase to a special meaning, *i.e.*, 'lust no sooner had is

hated past reason,' whereas it also means 'lust no sooner had *past reason* is hated past reason.' The comma might as well have been put between *reason* and *hated;* it would have limited the meaning but no more than has been done." The last sentence here is illegitimate persuasion, and the preceding statement is much ado about nothing; for it is clear that if something is "Past reason hunted and . . . had" it is had past reason. They are trying to make ll. 6–7 needlessly repetitious.

[48] *Ibid.,* p. 69.

[49] *Ibid.,* p. 71. Their remarks are based on l. 11 of the Q text ("A blisse in proofe and proud and very wo") which is universally emended to *prov'd a* on very solid grounds: interchange of *u* and *v*, analogy with ll. 6 and 7 and l. 12, and commonplaces on the subject, e.g., Ralegh's "So fond Desire when it attaines, / The life expires, the woe remaines."

[50] *Ibid.,* p. 72.

[51] Cf. ll. 8–9 of Sonnet 148. The Quarto reads "Loves eye is not so true as all mens: no, / How can it?" Pooler accepts it with minor changes, and so does W. J. Craig in the Oxford Shakespeare. But in our text Rollins chooses to stress the pun in l. 8: "Love's eye is not so true as all men's no. / How can it?" However, here the Quarto text, or some version of it, is preferable to Rollins', for this is another case in which the sense of the line as a unit is subordinate to the meaning required by its relation to the next line.

[52] Cf. also Donne's "Elegy XIX," ll. 20 ff.

CHAPTER 5.

[1] See Leslie Hotson, *Shakespeare's Sonnets Dated and Other Essays* (New York, 1949), pp. 21 ff., hereafter cited as Hotson. It is clear from his loose notions of evidence and reasoning that in his dating of the Sonnets Hotson doesn't have a leg to stand on. In any case his arguments have been demolished by Walter Stone, "Shakespeare and the Sad Augurs," *JEGP,* LII (1953), 457–479; F. W. Bateson, "Elementary, My Dear Hotson!" *Essays in Criticism,* I (1951), 81–88; and Alfred Harbage, "Dating Shakespeare's Sonnets," *Shakespeare Quarterly,* I (1950), 57–63, hereafter cited as Harbage.

[2] These obelisks were set up in St. Peter's Square and in three other piazzas in Rome. Whether or not they were a subject of discussion in England is quite problematical. Incidentally, Hotson may have gotten a lead on the pyramids from Tucker, ed., *The Sonnets of Shakespeare* (Cambridge, 1924), p. 200, hereafter cited as Tucker.

[3] Hotson, pp. 25–26.

[4] Harbage, pp. 62–63. His final comment on Sonnet 123 is, "That there was available for purposes of allusion in Shakespeare's immediate world of 1603, something *novel,* something *strange,* pyramids built up with *newer might* from old models and therefore mere *dressings* of the originals, seems indisputable" (p. 63).

[5] Knights, *Explorations* (New York, 1947), p. 79, hereafter cited as

Knights. He paraphrases the first and second quatrains continuously in two different versions labeled *Sense 1* and *Sense 2*, but it is convenient to separate the readings of each quatrain.

[6] In Hotson's interpretation "strange" plays on the sense foreign, of another country.

[7] Besides sharing "dressing" (in different functions), Sonnets 76 and 123 share the rimes change-strange and old-told. Sonnet 76 deals with constancy of style because of a constant argument.

[8] Randle Cotgrave, *A Dictionarie of the French and English Tongues* (facs. of 1611 ed., Columbia, S.C., 1950), gives the following definition of *dresser:* "To straighten, set right, make straight, leuell, euen; also, to raise, aduance, erect; lift, set, hold, or take up; also, to direct, instruct, order, gouerne, traine up; to fashion; frame, build, make."

[9] Knights, pp. 79–80. The brackets are his.

[10] Wyndham, *The Poems of Shakespeare* (London, 1898), p. cxxviii, hereafter cited as Wyndham: "here, in a magnificent hyperbole, he asserts that 'pyramids' (l. 2) built up by Time with a might which is 'newer' by comparison to his own changelessness, are, for all their antiquity, but 'new dressings' of sights familiar to ante-natal existence. . . ."

[11] Tucker, pp. 200–201. Cf. Jordan's interpretation of l. 2, summarized in Alden, *The Sonnets of Shakespeare* (Boston, 1916), p. 288; cf. also the queries re l. 2 in Dowden, *The Sonnets of William Shakespere* (London, 1881), p. 283, hereafter cited as Dowden.

[12] It is generally a form of eternizing, as it is in Drayton, Sonnet 55, and the Whitney emblem. The latter (quoted in Henry Green, *Shakespeare and the Emblem Writers* [London, 1870], pp. 443–444) pictures the fall or overthrow of large buildings while books remain unharmed; beneath the picture is the following poem:

> If mightie Troie, with gates of steele, and brasse,
> Be worne awaie, with tracte of stealinge time:
> If Carthage raste: if Thebes be grown with grasse.
> If Babel stoope: that to the clouds did clime:
> If Athens, and Numantia suffered spoile:
> If Aegypt spires, be evened with the soile.

> Then, what maye laste, which time dothe not impeache,
> Since that wee see, theise monuments are gone:
> Nothinge at all, but time doth over reache,
> It eates the steele, and weares the marble stone:
> But writinges laste, thoughe yt doe what it can,
> And are preserved, even since the worlde began.

> And so they shall, while that they same dothe laste,
> Which have declar'd, and shall to future age:
> What thinges before three thousand yeares have paste,
> What martiall knightes, have march'd upon this stage:
> Whose actes, in bookes if writers did not save,
> Their fame had ceaste, and gone with them to grave.

164

Of Samsons strength, of worthie Josuas might.
Of Davids actes, of Alexanders farce.
Of Caesar greate; and Scipio noble knight,
Howe shoulde we speake, but bookes thereof discourse:
Then favour them, that learne within their youthe:
But love them beste, that learne, and write the truth.
Cf. Daniel's *Musophilus* (1599), ll. 306–396; Horace's *Exegi monumentum*, ll. 1–2; Ovid's *Metamorphoses*, XV.871 ff.

[13] Lever, *The Elizabethan Love Sonnet* (London, 1956), includes Sonnet 123 in the immortalization group and reads it (as he does most of his group) in terms of passages in *Metamorphoses*, XV.

[14] Knights, p. 79. Beeching, *The Sonnets of Shakespeare* (Boston, 1904), p. 121, hereafter cited as Beeching, points out that ll. 5–6 are "an expansion of line 4."

[15] Dowden, p. 283.

[16] Wyndham, pp. cxxviii–cxxxix.

[17] Knights's version (p. 80) of Wyndham's reading of the second quatrain is as follows: "Man's life is short; therefore he tends to wonder at the antiquities foisted upon him by Time, preferring to accept as absolute the limitations imposed by birth and death [to make them (dates) the bourn to his desire] than to think that the years of his life have been counted [told] before."

[18] The orthodox reading of l. 8 makes sense when combined with Wyndham's reading of l. 7, but there is the grammatical difficulty of "them" referring to "dates" (l. 7) and to "what thou dost foist" (l. 8).

[19] Johnson, *The Rambler*, No. 137.

[20] Cf. ll. 9–12 of Sonnet 116 with the couplet of 123. Somewhat different readings of ll. 9–14 of 123 are offered by Knights (p. 80), Hotson (p. 26), and Beeching (p. 121).

[21] Tucker, pp. 201–202.

[22] Cf. the use of "no" in Sonnets 121, 123, and 125.

[23] Late in the second book of *The Advancement of Learning*, Bacon devotes quite a few pages to discussing the "architecture of fortune" or the philosophy of getting ahead in the world.

[24] Pooler, *The Works of Shakespeare: Sonnets*, 3rd ed. (London, 1943), p. 119, hereafter cited as Pooler. Cf. the third stanza of Ralegh's "Conceipt Begotten by the Eyes":

Affection followes Fortunes wheels;
And soone is shaken from her heeles;
For following beautie or estate,
Hir liking still is turn'd to hate.
For all affections haue their change,
And fancie onely loues to range.

[25] In the first reading "as" denotes according as or since; in the second, just as.

[26] Cf. *Shakespeare's Sonnets* (New York, 1936), p. 326, hereafter cited as Brooke, and also Dowden's view, p. 284.

[27] Pooler, p. 119.

[28] H.V. IV.i.260–269.

[29] "Thrallèd discontent" may also mean discontent held under control or in subjection. Many commentators see political allusions here,

but nothing specific can be discerned. Hotson (pp. 27 ff.) sees in ll. 6–7 an allusion to the murder of Henry of Valois, king of France.

[30] Brooke, p. 326.

[31] Pooler, p. 120.

[32] Tyler, *Shakespeare's Sonnets* (London, 1890), p. 283. He is of course thinking of the etymology of "politic" (πόλις, city; state) as well as the context.

[33] Cf. "*drown* an eye (unused to flow)" in Sonnet 30.

[34] Arthur Mizener gives this definition of "for" in "The Structure of Figurative Language in Shakespeare's Sonnets," *Southern Review*, V (1939–1940), 745, hereafter cited as Mizener. The whole page (745) is against his definition, which makes l. 14 needlessly repetitious.

[35] Obviously I cannot accept Mizener's final remarks on Sonnet 124: "The most astonishing consequence of this line [14] is its inclusion among the fools of Time of the author of this sonnet, so that by a terrifying twist of irony Shakespeare offers his own failure—the unavoidable fact that, for all he has been saying about it, his love cannot escape the consequences of his being human and not divine—as part of the evidence for the truth of his contention that his love is not the child of state" (pp. 745–746). The whole weight of the Sonnet (and of Sonnets 123 and 125) is against this statement.

The couplet, especially in view of such earlier words as "thrallèd discontent," "Policy," and "heretic," may seem to contain an allusion to religious or political martyrs, conspirators who were caught and executed; but the reference is very general, and nothing specific can be discovered.

[36] *The Whole Works of Jeremy Taylor,* ed. Reginald Heber (London, 1839), XI, 327.

[37] *Oth.* I.i.42–65. My italics emphasize words that are also found in the Sonnet, and a phrase recalling one in the poem. Shakespeare uses "extern" only twice, here and in Sonnet 125.

Incidentally, another passage in *Othello* (II.i.13–19), describing the storm which threatens the Turkish fleet, clarifies l. 12 of Sonnet 116. Both the passage and the poem contain sea imagery and the words "ever-fixed" and "bear it out." When Shakespeare in 116 says that "Love . . ./ . . . bears it out even to the edge of doom," he is not only saying that it survives or endures; he is resuming the imagery of the second quatrain and claiming that it weathers the storm, the "tempests" of l. 6.

[38] See Dowden, p. 285; Pooler, p. 121; Brooke, p. 327.

[39] Dowden, p. 285. Cf. Beeching, Wyndham, Tucker, and Adams.

[40] Nashe uses a similar metaphor in speaking of informers currying favor: "that thereby they may lay the foundation to build a suit on." Quoted in J. D. Wilson, ed., *Life in Shakespeare's England* (Harmondsworth, Eng., 1944), p. 194, hereafter cited as Wilson.

[41] *H.VIII.* III.ii.367–373. Leishman, *Themes and Variations in Shakespeare's Sonnets* (London, 1961), p. 113, offers this paraphrase of the first quatrain: "Could it mean anything to me if I had merely given external expression in my verse to my admiration for your external appearance, and if the eternity which I claimed both for my love and

for my verse had been based upon anything so transient as this?" It represents a variation on the standard view and is not quite satisfactory.

[42] Beeching, p. 122. Rollins quotes him in the notes to our text. Cf. also Tucker, p. 205.

[43] "Sticklers for" is Onions' definition.

[44] John Lyly to Queen Elizabeth, quoted in Wilson, pp. 183–184. Cf. *Cym.* V.iv.127–129: "Poor wretches, that depend / On greatness' favour dream as I have done; / Wake, and find nothing."

[45] The syntax of ll. 6–7 is ambiguous; our text makes each line a more or less independent unit of sense, but the Quarto combines them: "Lose all, and more by paying too much rent / For compound sweet; Forgoing simple savor." As far as I can see, the difference is chiefly one of emphasis.

[46] With the octave of 125 cf. ll. 1–8 of Sonnet 25:

> Let those who are in favor with their stars
> Of public honor and proud titles boast,
> Whilst I, whom fortune of such triumph bars,
> Unlooked for joy in that I honor most.
> Great princes' favorites their fair leaves spread
> But as the marigold at the sun's eye;
> And in themselves their pride lies burièd,
> For at a frown they in their glory die.

[47] As Jeremy Taylor says, "Humility and charity are the two greatest graces in the world; and these are the greatest ingredients, which constitute friendship and express it" (*Works*, XI, 318).

[48] Steevens is quoted in *Variorum*, I, 317. Wyndham (pp. cxxxii, 324) offers a perverse alternative.

[49] Cf. Iago's use of "second" a few lines before his long speech quoted above: "Preferment goes by letter and affection, / Not by the old gradation, where each second / Stood heir to the first" (*Oth.* I.i.36–38).

[50] Cf. "take / No stricter render of me than my all" (*Cym.* V.iv.6–7); "Lady, as you are mine, I am yours: I give away myself for you and dote upon the exchange" (*Much* II.i.321–322); and *A Lover's Complaint* (ll. 218–224):

> Lo! all these trophies of affections hot,
> Of pensiv'd and subdu'd desires the tender,
> Nature hath charg'd me that I hoard them not,
> But yield them up where I myself must *render,*
> That is, to you, my origin and ender;
> For these, of force, must your *oblations* be,
> Since I their altar, you enpatron me.

Cf. also Eph. 6:5–6 (quoted in Luther's *Short Catechism*), with its emphasis on serving in singleness of heart from the heart, "not with service to the eye."

In view of ll. 9–10 as well as l. 12, there may be a suggestion of the "exchange of hearts" conceit in the third quatrain; cf. Sonnets 22 and 24.

[51] Quoted in Wilson, p. 194.

⁵² *Venus and Adonis*, ll. 649–655. Note the resemblance to Nashe's comments on informers. Incidentally, another candidate for the suborned informer might be Policy.

CHAPTER 6.

¹ See, for example, Sonnets 91, 92, 93 (discussed on pp. 16–17 above); 33, 34, 35, (pp. 57–59); 53, 54, 55 (p. 45); 118, 119, 120. Of course some Sonnets like 57 and 58, 135 and 136 are not related in sequence. The relationship of poems in sequence suggests that they may well stand in their order of composition.

² Brooke, *Shakespeare's Sonnets* (New York, 1936), pp. 19–24, sketches and illustrates three kinds of linking: syntactic, echoic (word, phrase, or idea), and thematic.

³ "O'ersways" occurs once in the Sonnets, "sway" twice—here and in 150 (65 and 66 unrelated); "beggar" and "beggared" once (66 and 67 related); 121 and 122 not related; "record" occurs four times (122 and 123 probably related); "render" occurs only in 125 and 126, which are not related. Since 121 ends a group and 123 is related to 124 and 125 and perhaps to 122, all this suggests that 121–126 are in the right order.

⁴ E. K. Chambers, "Shakespeare," *Encyclopedia Britannica* (Chicago, 1957), XX, 444.

⁵ I reproduce the groupings of Alden, *The Sonnets of Shakespeare* (Boston, 1916), p. 431, and Tucker, *The Sonnets of Shakespeare* (Cambridge, 1924), p. lxi, for comparison.
Alden: 1–17; 18–19; 26–28; 33–35; 40–42; 43–45; 46–47; 50–52; 54–55; 56–58; 63–65; 66–68; 69–70; 71–74; 78–80; 82–86; 87–93; 94–96; 97–99; 100–103; 109–112; 117–120; 123–125; 131–132; 133–134; 135–136; 137–138; 139–140; 141–142; 143–144; 147–152; 153–154.
Tucker: °I–XVII, XVIII–XIX, °XXVII–XXVIII, °XXX–XXXI, °XXXIII–XXXIV (and probably XXXV), XXXVIII–XXXIX, °XL–XLII, °XLIV–XLV, °XLVI–XLVII, °L–LI, LVI (perhaps with) °LVII–LVIII, LXIII (apparently with) °LXIV–LXV, °LXVI–LXVIII, °LXXI–LXXII, °LXXIII–LXXIV, °LXXVIII–LXXX, °LXXXII–LXXXVI, LXXXVII (apparently with) °LXXXVIII–XC, °XCI–XCIII, XCIV–XCVI, XCVII–XCIX, C–CI (connected in theme with) CII–CIII, CIX (with) °CX–CXII, °CXIII–CXIV, °CXVII–CXIX (perhaps with CXX), CXXIII (apparently with) °CXXIV–CXXV. The ° denotes what Tucker calls the "more certain groupings."

⁶ Some Sonnets, however, are independent and virtually unique (66, 129, 146, for example), and the Sonnets are full of things not found in the plays.

⁷ *Elizabethan Critical Essays*, ed. G. Gregory Smith, 2 vols. (London, 1904), II, 288.

⁸ Empson probably acquired some of his approaches to the Sonnets, including his eye for ambiguous syntax, from Riding and Graves. Unfortunately, some of his examples are trivial and artificial (v. chap. iii, n. 55, above), just as some of theirs are. Much of his criticism

is very intelligent and sensitive, but I must agree with Knights that in Empson's analyses of the Sonnets "his lists of meanings seem . . . to be obtained by focussing upon a part of the poem, almost one might say by forgetting the poem, and considering the various grammatical possibilities of the part so isolated." *Explorations* (New York, 1947), p. 73.

⁹ See B. F. Skinner, "The Verbal Summator and a Method for the Study of Latent Speech," *Journal of Psychology*, II (1936), 71–107; E. A. Armstrong, *Shakespeare's Imagination* (London, 1946), especially chap. 13, "Streamy Associations."

¹⁰ Empson, *Seven Types of Ambiguity*, 2nd ed. (Norfolk, Conn., 1947), p. 138; cf. *ibid.*, pp. 87–88. See also E. E. Kellett's intelligent essay in *Suggestions* (Cambridge, 1923), "Some Notes on a Feature of Shakespere's Style," esp. pp. 58–59, 69, and 74–75.

¹¹ J. Dover Wilson, ed., *Hamlet* (Cambridge, 1936), p. xxxv.

¹² T. S. Eliot, *The Use of Poetry and the Use of Criticism* (London, 1933), pp. 146–147. There are echoes of Coleridge's *Table Talk* in this passage.

¹³ See R. M. Alden, "The Lyrical Conceit of the Elizabethans," *Studies in Philology*, XIV (1917), 149, n. 20.

¹⁴ Ransom condemns Shakespeare for being a romantic rather than a metaphysical poet in the Sonnets and for not adapting the logic of his poems to their metrical pattern. His views are set forth in an acute essay entitled "Shakespeare at Sonnets," first published in *The Southern Review*, III (1938), 531–553, and reprinted in *The World's Body* (New York, 1938). Mizener's analysis of Sonnet 124, in "The Structure of Figurative Language in Shakespeare's Sonnets," *Southern Review*, V (1940), 730–747, contains a refutation of Ransom's chief dogmas.

¹⁵ Yvor Winters, *On Modern Poets* (New York, 1959), p. 127. Coleridge (in the epigraph to the chapter) and Eliot have already "answered" Winters' objection. Incidentally, it has always been evident that Winters prefers poetry which is rational and denotational, a classical poetry of moral statement; see, for example, his valuable essay in reinterpretation, "The 16th Century Lyric in England," *Poetry*, LIII (1939), 258–272, 320–335; LIV (1939), 35–51.

¹⁶ Northrop Frye, *Anatomy of Criticism* (Princeton, 1957), p. 281. In the next sentence he says, "Much more frequently than any other genre does the lyric depend for its main effect on the fresh or surprising image, a fact which often gives rise to the illusion that such imagery is radically new or unconventional." Both statements require some qualification.

¹⁷ The diagram is only a crude schema suggesting some main lines of association; however, it does indicate how almost all the distinctive words and figures could grow out of the first line.

¹⁸ T. W. Baldwin, *On the Literary Genetics of Shakespere's Poems & Sonnets* (Urbana, Ill., 1950), p. 350.

¹⁹ C. S. Lewis, *English Literature in the Sixteenth Century* (Oxford, 1954), p. 506. He gives some brief analyses on p. 507.

²⁰ *Ibid.*, p. 508. With the first sentence compare G. K. Hunter's "The Dramatic Technique of Shakespeare's Sonnets," *Essays in Criticism*,

III (1953), 152–164. With the last two sentences compare Winifred Nowottny's valuable but uneven essay, "Formal Elements in Shakespeare's Sonnets I–VI," *Essays in Criticism*, II (1952), 76–84.

[21] F. W. Bateson, *English Poetry and the English Language* (Oxford, 1934), pp. 63–64. (He attributes the diffuseness and repetitions of Elizabethan style to a fear of change in language [pp. 31–32] and remarks that the diffuseness of Elizabethan poetry was imposed on the poets by the high proportion of "new or partially assimilated words they were compelled to use" [p. 34].) The second sentence in the quotation is very careless: "add" and "original meaning" (like his later writings on poetry) stress the sense or denotation of poetry and are needlessly vague. He is talking as if all poets wrote like Ben Jonson—from a prose version of what they intended to "say."

[22] Claes Schaar decisively refutes Baldwin's assertions in the "Structure" section of *An Elizabethan Sonnet Problem*, pp. 27–37, hereafter cited as Schaar. After quoting the passage summarizing Baldwin's views he says (p. 28), "This emphatic assertion . . . does not cover the actual facts. A detailed examination of the structure of the Shakespearean sonnets, on the contrary, shows that the poet conforms to this system in its pure form in less than a tenth of the sonnets, and to some modification of it in less than a quarter. . . ."

[23] Josephine Miles, *Eras and Modes in English Poetry* (Berkeley and Los Angeles, 1957), pp. 1–19, hereafter cited as Miles.

[24] Cf. Wyndham's analysis of the sound and rhythm of Sonnet 1 in *The Poems of Shakespeare* (London, 1898), pp. cxlii–cxliv.

[25] Miles, p. 14. She quotes a Wyatt sonnet to exemplify the clausal mode, a Spenser sonnet to illustrate the phrasal.

[26] In the order of frequency within their class (noun, adjective, verb) the most frequent words are "love," "eye," "time," "beauty," "heart," "day," "thought," "world," and "death"; "sweet," "far," and "true"; "make," "live," "give," "see," "say," "know," "love," and "lie." (I have not separated the noun and verb uses of "love" and "lie," but "love"—by far the most frequent word—is usually a noun and "lie" a verb.) Except for "say" and "death," all these words appear in Miss Miles's list of main words (those most used by four or more poets) for 1570–1600.

[27] Schaar's conclusions in *An Elizabethan Sonnet Problem*—that the sonnets of Daniel and Shakespeare are fundamentally unlike in every respect and Daniel had no influence on Shakespeare—are valuable for demolishing a harmful academic myth, but they only tell the careful reader what he already knew.

[28] Cf. Theodore Redpath, ed., *The Song and Sonnets of John Donne* (London, 1956), pp. xli–xlii, and J. B. Leishman, *The Monarch of Wit*, 3rd ed. (London, 1957), pp. 227–228. Incidentally, Miss Miles's statistics help to point up the differences between Shakespeare and Donne, Shakespeare and Daniel.

Selected Bibliography

I. EDITIONS OF SHAKESPEARE'S SONNETS AND WORKS.

Alden, Raymond M., ed., *The Sonnets of Shakespeare* (Boston: Houghton Mifflin, 1916).

Baldensperger, Fernand, trans. and ed., *Les Sonnets de Shakespeare* (Berkeley and Los Angeles: University of California Press, 1943).

Beeching, H. C., ed., *The Sonnets of Shakespeare* (Boston, 1904).

Boswell, James, ed., *The Plays and Poems of William Shakespeare* (The 3rd Variorum, Boswell's Malone), 21 vols. (London, 1821).

Brooke, C. F. Tucker, ed., *The Shakespeare Apocrypha* (Oxford: Clarendon Press, 1908).

————, ed., *Shakespeare's Sonnets* (New York: Oxford University Press, 1936).

Craig, W. J., ed., *The Complete Works of William Shakespeare* (London: Oxford University Press, 1904).

Dowden, Edward, ed., *The Sonnets of William Shakespere* (London, 1881).

Harrison, G. B., ed., *William Shakespeare: The Sonnets and a Lover's Complaint* (The Penguin Shakespeare), rev. ed. (Harmondsworth, Eng.: Penguin Books, 1949).

Hubler, Edward, ed., *Shakespeare's Songs and Poems* (New York: McGraw-Hill, Inc., 1959).

Kittredge, George L., ed., *The Complete Works of Shakespeare* (Boston: Ginn, 1936).

Neilson, William A., and Charles J. Hill, eds., *The Complete Plays and Poems of William Shakespeare* (Boston: Houghton Mifflin, 1942)

Pooler, C. Knox, ed., *The Works of Shakespeare: Sonnets* (The

Arden Shakespeare), 3rd ed. (London: Methuen, 1943).

Reed, Edward B., ed., *Shakespeare's Sonnets* (The Yale Shakespeare) (New Haven: Yale University Press, 1923).

Ridley, M. R., ed., *Sonnets* (The New Temple Shakespeare) (London: J. M. Dent, 1934).

Rollins, Hyder E., ed., *A New Variorum Edition of Shakespeare: The Sonnets*, 2 vols. (Philadelphia: J. B. Lippincott, 1944).

———, ed., *William Shakespeare: Sonnets* (Crofts Classics) (New York: Appleton-Century-Crofts, 1951).

Shakespere's Sonnets, introd. by Thomas Tyler (Shakespere-Quarto Facsimiles, No. 30) (London: C. Praetorius, n.d.).

Tucker, T. G., ed., *The Sonnets of Shakespeare* (Cambridge, Eng.: Cambridge University Press, 1924).

Tyler, Thomas, ed., *Shakespeare's Sonnets* (London, 1890).

Walsh, C. M., ed., *Shakespeare's Complete Sonnets* (London: F. T. Unwin, 1908).

Wilson, John Dover, ed., *Hamlet* (Cambridge, Eng.: Cambridge University Press, 1936).

Wyndham, George, ed., *The Poems of Shakespeare* (London, 1898).

II. Other Books and Articles.

Omitted are such familiar reference works as the *O.E.D.*, Schmidt's lexicon, the glossaries of Onions and Dyce, Bartlett's concordance, and the grammars of Franz and Abbott.

Adams, Joseph Q., *A Life of William Shakespeare* (Boston: Houghton Mifflin, 1923).

Alden, Raymond M., "The Lyrical Conceit of the Elizabethans," *Studies in Philology*, XIV (1917), 129–152.

———, *Shakespeare* (New York: Duffield, 1922).

Alexander, Peter, *Shakespeare's Punctuation* (British Academy Lecture) (London: Oxford University Press, 1945).

Aquinas, St. Thomas, *Basic Writings*, ed. Anton G. Pegis, 2 vols. (New York: Random House, 1945).

Aristotle, *The Works Translated into English*, ed. W. D. Ross, 12 vols. (Oxford: Clarendon Press, 1908–1952).

———, *The Art of Rhetoric*, trans. John H. Freese (Loeb Library) (Cambridge, Mass.: Harvard University Press, 1926).

Armstrong, Edward A., *Shakespeare's Imagination* (London: Lindsay Drummond, 1946).

Babb, Lawrence, *The Elizabethan Malady* (East Lansing, Mich.: Michigan State College Press, 1951).

Bacon, Francis, *Essays and Colours of Good and Evil*, ed. W. Aldis Wright (London: Macmillan, 1867).

172

————, *The Advancement of Learning,* ed. William Aldis Wright, 5th ed. (Oxford: Clarendon Press, 1900).

Baldwin, T. W., *On the Literary Genetics of Shakespeare's Poems & Sonnets* (Urbana, Ill.: University of Illinois Press, 1950).

Bateson, F. W., *English Poetry and the English Language* (Oxford: Clarendon Press, 1934).

————, "Elementary, My Dear Hotson!" *Essays in Criticism,* I (1951), 81–88.

Browne, Sir Thomas, *Works,* ed. Simon Wilkin, 4 vols. (London, 1836).

Burton, Robert, *The Anatomy of Melancholy,* ed. A. R. Shilleto, 3 vols. (London, 1893).

Calvin, John, *The Institution of Christian Religion,* trans. Thomas Norton (London, 1611).

————, *Institutes of the Christian Religion,* trans. John Allen, 7th American ed., 2 vols. (Philadelphia: Presbyterian Board of Christian Education, 1936).

Campbell, Lily B., *Shakespeare's Tragic Heroes* (New York: Barnes and Noble, 1960).

Carter, Albert H., "The Punctuation of Shakespeare's *Sonnets* of 1609," *Joseph Quincy Adams Memorial Studies,* eds. J. G. McManaway *et al.* (Washington, D.C.: Folger Shakespeare Library, 1948). Pp. 409–428.

Chambers, Edmund K., "William Shakespeare," *Encyclopaedia Britannica* (Chicago, 1929).

————, *William Shakespeare, A Study of Facts and Problems,* 2 vols. (Oxford: Clarendon Press, 1930).

————, *Shakespearean Gleanings* (London: Oxford University Press, 1944).

Chaucer, Geoffrey, *The Works,* ed. F. N. Robinson, 2nd ed. (Boston: Houghton-Mifflin, 1957).

Cicero, *De Officiis,* trans. Walter Miller (Loeb Library) (Cambridge, Mass.: Harvard University Press, 1913).

Coleridge, Samuel Taylor, *Specimens of the Table Talk,* ed. H. N. Coleridge, 2 vols. (London, 1835).

————, *Aids to Reflection,* ed. H. N. Coleridge (Burlington, Vt., 1840).

————, *Biographia Literaria* (Bohn's Standard Library) (London: George Bell, 1905).

————, *Shakespearean Criticism,* ed. T. M. Raysor, 2 vols. (Cambridge, Mass.: Harvard University Press, 1930).

————, *Miscellaneous Criticism,* ed. T. M. Raysor (Cambridge, Mass.: Harvard University Press, 1936).

Cormican, L. A., "Medieval Idiom in Shakespeare: (I) Shakespeare and the Liturgy," *Scrutiny,* XVII (1950), 186–202.

De Sanctis, Francesco, *History of Italian Literature,* trans.

Joan Redfern, 2 vols. (New York: Harcourt, Brace, 1931).

Donne, John, *The Poems*, ed. Herbert Grierson (London: Oxford University Press, 1933).

——, *The Songs and Sonnets*, ed. Theodore Redpath (London: Methuen, 1956).

Eliot, T. S., *Selected Essays, 1917–1932* (New York: Harcourt, Brace, 1932).

——, *The Use of Poetry and the Use of Criticism* (London: Faber and Faber, 1933).

Elizabethan Critical Essays, ed. G. Gregory Smith, 2 vols. (London: Oxford University Press, 1904).

Elizabethan Sonnets, ed. Sidney Lee (An English Garner), 2 vols. (New York: E. P. Dutton, 1904).

Empson, William, *Some Versions of Pastoral* (London: Chatto and Windus, 1935).

——, *Seven Types of Ambiguity*, 2nd ed. (Norfolk, Conn.: New Directions, 1947).

——, *The Structure of Complex Words* (Norfolk, Conn.: New Directions, n.d.)

England's Helicon, ed. Hyder E. Rollins, 2 vols. (Cambridge, Mass.: Harvard University Press, 1935).

English Madrigal Verse, 1588–1632, ed. E. H. Fellowes, 2nd ed. (Oxford: Clarendon Press, 1929).

Erasmus, Desiderius, *The Praise of Folly*, trans. Leonard Dean (Chicago: Packard, 1946).

Fries, Charles C., "Shakespearian Punctuation," *Studies in Shakespeare, Milton, and Donne* (New York: Macmillan, 1925). Pp. 67–86.

Frye, Northrop, *Anatomy of Criticism* (Princeton, N.J.: Princeton University Press, 1957).

Gérard, Albert S., "The Stone as Lily: A Discussion of Shakespeare's Sonnet XCIV," *Shakespeare Jahrbuch*, 96 (1960), 155–160.

Goldsmith, U. K., "Words Out of a Hat? Alliteration and Assonance in Shakespeare's Sonnets," *Journal of English and Germanic Philology*, XLIX (1950), 33–48.

Gordon, George, *Shakespeare's English*, Society for Pure English Tract No. XXIX (Oxford: Clarendon Press, 1928).

Green, Henry, *Shakespeare and the Emblem Writers* (London, 1870).

Harbage, Alfred, "Dating Shakespeare's Sonnets," *Shakespeare Quarterly*, I (1950), 57–63.

Hotson, Leslie, *Shakespeare's Sonnets Dated and Other Essays* (New York: Oxford University Press, 1949).

174

————, *Shakespeare's Motley* (London: Rupert Hart-Davis, 1952).

Hubler, Edward, "Shakespeare's Sonnets Dated," *Shakespeare Quarterly*, I (1950), 78–83.

————, *The Sense of Shakespeare's Sonnets* (Princeton, N.J.: Princeton University Press, 1952).

Hunter, G. K., "The Dramatic Technique of Shakespeare's Sonnets," *Essays in Criticism*, III (1953), 152–164.

Kellett, E. E., *Suggestions* (Cambridge: Cambridge University Press, 1923).

King, Arthur H., "Some Notes on Ambiguity in *Henry IV* Part I," *Studia Neophilologica*, XIV (1941–1942), 161–183.

Knight, G. Wilson, *The Mutual Flame* (London: Methuen, 1955).

Knights, L. C., "Shakespeare's Sonnets," *Scrutiny*, III (1934), 133–160.

————, *Explorations* (New York: George W. Stewart, 1947).

Kristeller, Paul O., *The Classics and Renaissance Thought* (Cambridge, Mass.: Harvard University Press, 1955).

Lee, Sidney, *A Life of William Shakespeare* (London: Smith, Elder, 1915).

————, *Elizabethan and Other Essays*, ed. F. S. Boas (Oxford: Clarendon Press, 1929).

Leishman, J. B., *The Monarch of Wit*, 3rd ed. (London: Hutchinson, 1957).

————, *Themes and Variations in Shakespeare's Sonnets* (London: Hutchinson, 1961).

Lever, J. W., *The Elizabethan Love Sonnet* (London: Methuen, 1956).

Lewis, C. S., *English Literature in the Sixteenth Century* (Oxford: Clarendon Press, 1954).

Liturgical Services of the Reign of Queen Elizabeth, ed. William Clay (Parker Society) (Cambridge, Eng., 1847).

Luther, Martin, *Primary Works*, ed. Henry Wace and C. A. Buchheim (London, 1896).

Machiavelli, Niccolò, *The Prince and The Discourses*, trans. Luigi Ricci and C. E. Detmold (New York: Modern Library, 1940).

Mahood, M. M., *Shakespeare's Wordplay* (London: Methuen, 1957).

Marlowe, Christopher, *The Works*, ed. C. F. Tucker Brooke (Oxford: Clarendon Press, 1910).

Miles, Josephine, *Eras and Modes in English Poetry* (Berkeley and Los Angeles: University of California Press, 1957).

Mizener, Arthur, "The Structure of Figurative Language in

Shakespeare's Sonnets," *Southern Review*, V (1940), 730–747.

Mommsen, T. E., "Introduction," *Petrarch: Sonnets and Songs*, trans. A. M. Armi (New York: Pantheon Books, 1946).

Montaigne, Michel de, *The Essays*, trans. E. J. Trechmann, 2 vols. in 1 (New York: Oxford University Press, n.d.).

Noble, Richmond, *Shakespeare's Biblical Knowledge* (London: Society for Promoting Christian Knowledge, 1935).

Nosworthy, J. M. "All Too Short a Date: Internal Evidence in Shakespeare's Sonnets," *Essays in Criticism*, II (1952), 311–324.

Nowottny, Winifred, "Formal Elements in Shakespeare's Sonnets I–VI," *Essays in Criticism*, II (1952), 76–84.

Ong, Walter J., "Historical Backgrounds of Elizabethan and Jacobean Punctuation Theory," *PMLA*, LIX (1944), 349–360.

Ovid, *Metamorphoses*, trans. Frank Miller (Loeb Library), 2 vols. (London: William Heinemann, 1916, 1926).

Pettett, E. C., "Shakespeare's Conception of Poetry," *Essays and Studies*, III (1950), 29–46.

Plato, *The Republic*, trans. Francis M. Cornford (London: Oxford University Press, 1941).

Praz, Mario, *The Flaming Heart* (Garden City, N.Y.: Doubleday, 1958).

Ralegh, Sir Walter, *The History of the World* (London, 1687).

——, *The Poems*, ed. Agnes M. C. Latham (Muses Library) (Cambridge, Mass.: Harvard University Press, 1951).

Ransom, John Crowe, "Mr. Empson's Muddles," *Southern Review*, IV (1938), 322–339.

——, "Shakespeare at Sonnets," *Southern Review*, III (1938), 531–553.

——, *The World's Body* (New York: Charles Scribner's, 1938).

Richards, I. A., *Principles of Literary Criticism* (New York: Harcourt, Brace, 1926).

——, *Practical Criticism* (New York: Harcourt, Brace, 1929).

——, *The Philosophy of Rhetoric* (New York: Oxford University Press, 1936).

——, *How to Read a Page* (New York: W. W. Norton, 1942).

——, *Speculative Instruments* (London: Routledge and Kegan Paul, 1955).

Riding, Laura, and Robert Graves, *A Survey of Modernist Poetry* (New York: Doran, 1928).

Santayana, George, *Reason in Society* (New York, 1905).

Schaar, Claes, *An Elizabethan Sonnet Problem* (Lund Studies in English, XXVIII) (Lund, Sweden: C. W. K. Gleerup, 1960).

Schoen-René, Otto E., *Shakespeare's Sonnets in Germany* (*1787–1939*), Harvard University dissertation (1942).

Schultz, John H., "A Glossary of Shakespeare's Hawking Language," *University of Texas Studies in English* (1938), pp. 174–205.

Scott, Janet G., *Les sonnets élisabéthains* (Paris: H. Champion, 1929).

Selections from Medieval Philosophers, ed. Richard McKeon, 2 vols. (New York: Charles Scribner's, 1929–1930).

Sidney, Sir Philip, *Astrophel and Stella*, ed. Alfred Pollard (London, 1888).

Siegel, Paul N., "Petrarchan Sonneteers and Neo-Platonic Love," *Studies in Philology*, XLII (1945), 164–182.

———, "Sex and the Sonnet," *Essays in Criticism*, II (1952), 465–468.

Simpson, Percy, *Shakespearian Punctuation* (Oxford: Clarendon Press, 1911).

Sisson, C. J., *New Readings in Shakespeare*, 2 vols. (Cambridge: Cambridge University Press, 1956).

Skinner, B. F., "The Verbal Summator and a Method for the Study of Latent Speech," *Journal of Psychology*, II (1936), 71–107.

Smith, Hallett, *Elizabethan Poetry* (Cambridge, Mass.: Harvard University Press, 1952).

Spencer, Theodore, *Shakespeare and the Nature of Man* (New York: Macmillan, 1942).

Spenser, Edmund, *The Poetical Works*, ed. J. C. Smith and E. De Selincourt (London: Oxford University Press, 1912).

Stevenson, Charles L., *Ethics and Language* (New Haven, Conn.: Yale University Press, 1944).

The Stoic and Epicurean Philosophers, ed. Whitney J. Oates (New York: Random House, 1940).

Stone, Walter B., "Shakespeare and the Sad Augurs," *Journal of English and Germanic Philology*, LII (1953), 457–479.

Sypher, Wylie, "Shakespeare as Casuist," *Sewanee Review*, LVIII (1950), 262–280.

Tannenbaum, S. A., *The Handwriting of the Renaissance* (New York: Columbia University Press, 1930).

———, *Shakespere's Sonnets* (*A Concise Bibliography*) (New York: S. A. Tannenbaum, 1940).

Taylor, A. E., *Plato: The Man and His Work* (New York: Meridian Books, 1956).

Taylor, Jeremy, *The Whole Works,* ed. Reginald Heber, 15 vols. (London, 1839).

Tilley, Morris P., *A Dictionary of the Proverbs in England in the Sixteenth and Seventeenth Centuries* (Ann Arbor, Mich.: University of Michigan Press, 1950).

Traversi, D. A., *An Approach to Shakespeare,* 2nd ed. (Garden City, N.Y.: Doubleday, 1956).

The Two Liturgies . . . of King Edward VI, ed. Joseph Ketley (Parker Society) (Cambridge, Eng., 1844).

Van Doren, Mark, *Shakespeare* (New York: Henry Holt, 1939).

Watson, Curtis Brown, *Shakespeare and the Renaissance Concept of Honor* (Princeton, N.J.: Princeton University Press, 1960).

Whitaker, Virgil K., *Shakespeare's Use of Learning* (San Marino, Calif.: Huntington Library, 1953).

Wilson, F. P., *Shakespeare and the Diction of Common Life* (British Academy Lecture) (London: Oxford University Press, 1941).

Wilson, John Dover, ed., *Life in Shakespeare's England* (Harmondsworth, Eng.: Penguin Books, 1944).

Winters, Yvor, "The 16th Century Lyric in England," *Poetry,* LIII (1939), 258–272, 320–335; LIV (1939), 35–51.

————, *On Modern Poets* (New York: Meridian Books, 1959).

Wordsworth, William, *The Poetical Works,* ed. T. Hutchinson, rev. E. De Selincourt (London: Oxford University Press, 1904).

Wyatt, Sir Thomas, *Collected Poems,* ed. Kenneth Muir (Muses Library) (Cambridge, Mass.: Harvard University Press, 1950).

Index of Shakespeare's Works

SONNETS

Plays and poems

Index of Names and Subjects

Conrad, Joseph, 28
Corona, 143
Cotgrave, Randle, 164
Craig, W. J., 144, 163

Daniel, Samuel, 141, 165, 170
De Sanctis, F., 144
Donne, John, 99, 118, 135, 141, 143, 148, 150, 153, 162, 163, 170
Dowden, Edward, 13 ff., 22, 31, 67, 90, 110, 111, 122–123, 144, 145, 151, 155, 161–166 passim
Drayton, Michael, 109, 164
Dyce, Alexander, 2, 158–159

Eliot, T. S., 134–135, 141, 169
Elizabeth, Queen, 148, 167
Elizabethan sonnet sequence, 4, 144
Elyot, Sir Thomas, 161
Empson, William, 28, 78, 81, 133, 145, 149, 156, 158, 168–169
Epictetus, 21, 146
Erasmus, 77, 137, 153, 158
eros, 16, 126, 145
Essex, Earl of, 84, 85, 113
Euripides, 145

Fenollosa, Ernest, 140
Fool, 76 ff., 118–119, 158
Freud, Sigmund, 56
Frye, Northrop, 135–136, 169

Gérard, Albert S., 149
Green, Henry, 164
Greville, Fulke, 135

Harbage, Alfred, 107, 163
Harris, Frank, 157
Harrison, G. B., 146
Hoby, Sir Thomas, 28, 152
Horace, 165
Hotson, Leslie, 106–107, 163–166 passim
Hubler, Edward, 68, 150, 151, 156
Hunter, G. K., 169–170

Interpretation as comparison of contexts, 6, 38
Irony, 20

James, King, 107
Johnson, Samuel, 134, 146, 147, 165
Jonson, Ben, 135, 170

Kellett, E. E., 169
King, Arthur H., 149
Kittredge, G. L., 146
Knight, G. Wilson, 88, 90, 93, 107, 160, 161–162
Knights, L. C., 70–71, 81, 88, 107–111 passim, 144, 154–165 passim, 169
Kristeller, P. O., 152

Lee, Sidney, 108, 144
Leishman, J. B., 49, 149, 152, 166–167, 170
Lever, J. W., 32 ff., 39, 150, 151, 152, 165
Lewis, C. S., 54, 137–138, 139, 144, 153, 162, 169
Luther, Martin, 167
Lyly, John, 124–125, 167

Machiavelli, 95–96, 162
Mahood, M. M., 71–72, 157, 158
Malone, Edmund, 61
Marlowe, Christopher, 160
McKeon, R., 152
Miles, Josephine, 139–140, 170
Mizener, Arthur, 166, 169
Modes of English poetry, 139–140
Mommsen, T. E., 144
Montaigne, 155

Nashe, Thomas, 127, 166
Nature's gifts, 8, 9, 23–24, 83, 144–148 passim
Nowottny, Winifred, 170

Ong, Walter J., 147
Onions, C. T., 108, 127, 158, 162, 167
Ovid, 155, 165

183